COUNTIES
FRAME BODY
NO 7256

BARTON

34 WALES

URR 862

IING
ADE G

EASTERN COACH WORKS LTD
LOWESTOFT
BODY No 20799
THE ABOVE NUMBER SHOULD BE QUOTED ON
ALL ENQUIRIES REGARDING THIS BODY

cles.   Obviously their designers could not move outside the
appearance could be affected by the requirements of a large
control of one major shareholder his whims could spoil the

on; Strachans Successors, London; Plaxtons, Scarborough.
ough; Burlingham, Blackpool.

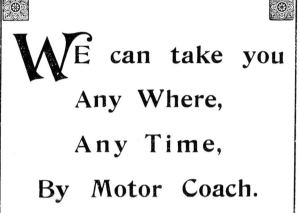

WE can take you
Any Where,
Any Time,
By Motor Coach.

Parties and Outings
Our
Speciality.

'Phone 443.

Epitomizing all that was good in the coaching world, in this photograph of June 1933 Burnell's (of Weston-super-Mare) smartly uniformed chauffeur stands in front of their Wycombe bodied Gilford, new that year. The board says it all! The domed objects below the headlights Gruss air springs, were adjustable according to the load carried.

1910
COACHING CAVALCADE
1970

David Gladwin

BREWIN BOOKS

First published November 1991 by
K.A.F. Brewin Books, Studley, Warwickshire. B80 7LG

ISBN 0 947731 71 7

Typeset in Baskerville 11pt by Supaprint (Redditch)Ltd.,
Printed and bound by
The Cromwell Press Limited,
Broughton Gifford, Melksham,
Wiltshire

ACKNOWLEDGEMENTS

Any book of this type involves some complicated, but interesting research. Even when this has been carefully carried out errors and omissions can occur but both author and publisher are glad to acknowledge that in no way can any mistakes or oversights be attributed to the various members of societies, staff or individuals who gave all possible assistance.

Archivist, Bolton Central Library; British Bus Preservation Group; Carlyle Bus Centre Ltd.; Alan B. Cross; Dennis Specialist Vehicles; East Pennine Transport Group; 2849 Group; Bob Harris, Wombourne; Edward Jacobs; Keith Jenkinson, Editor, Bus Fayre; Kevin Lane; R.C. Ludgate; John Marsh; Colin F. Martin; Newcastle City Libraries; Omnibus Society; G. Pickard; Plaxton Bus & Coach; P.S.V. Circle; G.A. Rixon; Royal Institute of Cornwall; Chris Terrington; Vectis Transport Publications; Willowbrook, Loughborough; Woodspring Museum, Weston-super-Mare.

The final acknowledgement must be to my wife, who isn't quite as keen on elderly coaches as I am, having all too vivid memories of the short commons we have had in the bad times. Nonetheless she is typist, filing clerk and all but joint writer, work carried out in between her own research and writing.

PHOTOGRAPHIC AND DOCUMENTARY ACKNOWLEDGEMENTS

We are pleased to acknowledge our thanks to the following for the use of photographs and documents. The balance are by the author or drawn from the author's collection - many are without any indication of source, and it has, therefore been impossible to trace the copyright holder.

G. Archer, Blackpool Transport Services; B. Mills, Local Studies Librarian, Bolton Reference Library; W.A. Camwell; M. Allan, Chiltern Queens Coaches; The Editor, Coaching Journal; The Editor, Coachmart; The Editor, Commercial Motor; The Curator, Royal Insititute of Cornwall, Truro; A. Gordon; W.J. Haynes; P. Higgs; E. Berry, Lancastrian Transport Publications; K. Lane; R.C. Ludgate; John Marsh; C.F. Martin; A. Meadows; G.R. Mills; F. Manders and Mrs. P. Sheldon, Local Studies Library, Newcastle-upon-Tyne Libraries & Arts; R.H.G. Simpson; W.G. Smith of Smiths Imperial Coaches; Jane Evans and Sharon Poole, Woodspring Museum, Weston-super-Mare; Judy-Joan Wright.

CONTENTS

INTRODUCTION

Rather than cause any confusion it is as well to state this is a book about coaches rather than buses and furthermore traditional British coaches at that. Our American cousins use the word 'bus' to define almost any Public Service Vehicle, whereas a bus service has, in Britain, a properly defined route from A to B stopping at various places and running to a timetable with clearly stated point-to-point fares covering all stopping places. A coach trip on the other hand, is usually advertised in a rather loosely defined way, thus 'Day trip to the Wye Valley' or, more clearly, 'Epsom for the Races', or the vaguest of them all, the 'Mystery Tour'. Passengers are picked up from, probably, two or three localities and the only booked intermediate breaks in the journey are, or were, 'comfort' stops.

The 'bus' vehicle by its nature was, and is, designed to get in as many passengers as possible, it offered minimal comfort and, too often, sacrificed interior trim to help gain better fuel consumption, whereas a coach was, almost invariably, single deck and had to provide a pleasant ambience for anything up to ten hours which would, the operator hoped, persuade the passengers to travel again by the same means.

But a coach tour (say one of Thomas Cook's costing £47.25 inclusive of everything, bar tips) could involve 1,600 miles travelling in 13 days but did not place the same requirements on the vehicle as a day trip. Reliability had to be spot-on for a week or two's work, particularly where timings were tight, whereas returning after a day-trip was not governed by a set time and it didn't matter if an overheated engine was nursed home. So at any one time a driver could see parked alongside another vehicle 20 or 30 years different in age, style and comfort.

Two grey areas appear, one is an 'Express' route which functioned as a fare-stage journey but involved far greater distances and required, at least, semi-coach seating albeit too often in a rather utilitarian body. The other was the sort of firm I knew best, who used other people's superannuated coaches on fare stage (bus) work partly because they were cheap, partly because they could, at a pinch, be used for day trips to the races, or the seaside, but mostly because our bus journeys took two or more hours for each route trundling around lanes and hamlets before arriving in town.

The period chosen - 1910–1970 - is quite deliberate. The char-a-bancs of 1910 differed little from then to 1925, except for improved tyres. The mid 1920s saw the heyday of the private owner until he was driven from the road by the infamous 1930 Road Traffic Act and thereafter the big companies outvied each other in producing more sumptious, more 'styled' coaches; the knock-on effect of this lasting until the time when the engine moved from alongside the driver to underneath the chassis and the era of the box began. Although the M1 was partially opened in November 1959, it was not until after 1970 the wholesale slaughter of 'real' coaches began. Today's coaching roads are a different world.

Within the parameters of the word 'coach' came many vehicular shapes and sizes therefore the illustrations in this book have been chosen to show the vehicle itself regardless of the duty it is performing. Just to confuse matters, at least two show real buses pretending to be coaches! One way in which we are lucky, photographically, is that in the pre-war motorway era there still survived - against all the laws of high finance - small, incredibly impecunious firms providing a service or services to almost depopulated villages and hamlets and these companies perforce ran antiquated vehicles which, fortunately, caught the photographers' eyes. Many of these routes ran only on Market Days, always spoken of in capital letters because they provided the bread, if no butter or margarine, for us. Saturday (pre-television) was the day for carrying courting couples and the like to the cinema or local clop-hopping dance (low carnel as one labourer called the Locarno) for their evenings entertainment 'up town'. Difficult though it may be to believe now we used to try to remember who was on the coach on the outward journey and if they were missing at the end send out a search party to bring them back for us to deliver them home albeit at the price of making everyone half-an-hour late.

When we operated our trundle around the villages our gaffers would have been unhappy had we not diverted up to Higgins Farm to collect our favourite pensioners, or stopped outside her door to pick up a disabled woman, Mary, or got "our Alice's" medicine from the chemist. The Traffic Commissioners, who agreed routes and fares, probably knew we broke the rules (as, indeed, we did) but as long as there were no complaints, who looked too hard? We carried newspapers, parcels, animals (four legged and a football team) we gave "Jennie, the Postie" complete with bag and bike, a lift in bad weather, waiting while she delivered to isolated farms. We had draughty, worn out coaches, we had windscreen wipers that either failed to function for lack of vacuum or froze to the windscreen, and our tyres didn't bear looking at. Sometimes we could not stop too well, although at least most of the companies I knew had a yard unlike a certain famous Derbyshire independent where I saw a gearbox changed on the grass verge (and none the worse for it). At other times we came to involuntary halts, and here was another side to the coin for if the driver could not repair whatever had broken - and we carried a wondrous supply of spare parts! - it was a poor farmer that couldn't either find the vital components, lend a knowledgeable tractor-driver to see what could be cobbled up or, at worse, drag us to the farm with a tractor (once complete with plough dangling in front of the windscreen) and telephone our gaffer. Mrs. Farmer would invariably get tea and scones for the passengers, conductor and driver alike.

For day trips come Spring-time, we would extract our secondhand AEC Regal, Albion Valiant, Dennis Lancet, Leyland PSI or whatever and any spare driver would quite cheerfully spend the Friday or Saturday evening polishing and cleaning the vehicle (albeit usually assisted by his current girl-friend) for with wood trim, moquette seats, carpeted floors and plenty of brass and chrome a little work could make our old nails really look attractive. The glass was cleaned inside and out, the old-fashioned 'jelly mould' light fittings taken down, cleaned and bulbs replaced where necessary, an antiquated 'Goblin' vacuum noisily but efficiently rooted about in the nooks and crannies, the radio (for had not these coaches been built in the era of 'Radio Coaches'?) was re-valved and generally prodded into life, everything that needed oiling was oiled, and greasing areas were greased. The bodywork, almost invariably, was by one of the ephemeral coach-building manufacturers that stopped making bits for aircraft rather hurriedly in 1945 and thought they'd build a few coaches. They were, of course, composite structures with a wooden frame, aluminium or steel skins, and what they lacked in rigidity often made up in either eccentric design or at least flashy trim; but then, it was the age of the Odeon Cinema and drivers who aspired to an Austin 10 or Hillman Minx rather than their GTii or XX99 Nipmobile of today. When our booking office (usually the Gaffer's daughter) opened up for business she didn't get asked for "four tickets to Lazarote or the Costa Whatta" but "four for our Margaret who wants the same as last year" or "For t'Wakes Week can us stay wi' Mrs. Pratt, cos our Albert didn't like Mrs. Collins' kippers". Talking to other, older, drivers from similar firms at Skeggy or Blackpool or

t'races or wherever, it seemed that coaching had always appealed to a certain type of passenger; good, honest, working men and women, many couldn't read, others probably had no running water or electricity at home. Thatched cottages all too often came with bed-bugs and sewage was "t'little house down t'garden". The girls used cheap perfume, had indescribable accents designed for use above the mill's clatter, but normally kept their virginity until they'd "gotten a chap"; the boys drank too much, fought occasionally, were eternal army privates and both sets were quite, quite, lost in a city.

It's all gone now, with only a few of these beautiful coaches preserved, the bus and coach services we ran have been superseded first by the television and then by the car. The grandchildren of our passengers are probably 'yuppies'; typically our hamlet, three miles from the village and seven from 'town' has one passenger vehicle a week, giving the pensioners just two hours for their shopping. I say passenger vehicle for ten years ago it was a Plaxton bodied Leyland Leopard, with coach seats, and now it is a converted mini-bread-van, rightly called a 'buzz' as everything about it rattles and squeaks.

On one trip many years ago I had our latest coach, about five years old, with a body manufactured by a firm called Bellhouse-Hartwell. We called it "the greenhouse" for the driver roasted in a massive glass bubble, but the seats next door to me were occupied by a honeymoon couple who had elected to join our tour for a week around Devon and Cornwall. It rained and rained and rained. On the Friday it stopped. On the Saturday we returned 240 miles back to base at a maximum legal speed of 30 mph. As the honeymoon couple got out the wife kissed me on the cheek and said words to the effect of "thank you for a lovely week, everyone has been so happy".

So in this book then let us join our honeymoon couple as they explore the coaching highways of Britain on a journey through time (1910-1970) and space (thousands of miles). For our time-machine we can use contemporary documents and photographs; we can only imagine the muted roar of our petrol engine and visualize that coaching aroma, a compound of wood, leather, moquette, beeswax polish and disinfectant (probably Jeyes Fluid) which we all knew so well. And if one day you are at a rally of old vehicles, think of the tales they could tell - many will have done a million miles in their lifetime and seen a million people.

Chapter One

Charabancs & Coaches

Classic coaching can be exemplified by the two vehicles on the facing page.

UY 1213, Samuel Johnson's latest vehicle in 1927, had a chassis built during a period of marketing and research co-operation between Daimler and AEC, the radiator header tank being embossed with the "Associated Daimler" mark. Commencing in 1926, this 416 type was the first true 'neutral' chassis, with AEC building this particular one, although the Daimler 423 was almost identical. About 1,000 416 were sold, powered by either an AEC 5.1 litre 4-cylinder engine of 45 h.p. at 1,000 rpm, or the Daimler equivalent of a 3.568 litre six cylinder model giving 70 h.p., at a rather disastrous 3,000 rpm.

Bodywork was dual purpose as with the windows dropped into the panelling and the hood furled an excellent tourer was available - at a maximum 20 mph draughts hardly mattered, but with the all-weather equipment in place it was claimed that saloon comfort was attainable. The ADC partnership was dissolved in July 1928. Heath Lane, Stourbridge, is part of the very busy B4186 connecting the A.491 and A.451 roads. You could not imitate Mr. Johnson's action today and photograph a new coach!

Also using woodland as a background, this Albion 'Valkyrie' coach of A & R Graham Ltd., Kerr Street, Kirkintilloch, was a 32 seater built in 1938 to the latest idiom. Classed by the manufacturers as a CX13 model SN 8565 had a six-cylinder oil engine of 9.08 litres. Built at Scotstoun, near Glasgow it was the logical chassis choice for Grahams. Although to modern eyes accustomed to cubist coaches the lines of the body look disjointed, none the less the finish and workmanship of the Martin Coachworks 32-seater vehicle are unlikely to be attained today. Sold with the business to Alexanders in July 1938, when the vehicle was less than a month old, SN8565 by then E29 in the Alexander fleet was withdrawn in July 1944, but in other ownership served until 1953, a testimonial to both chassis and body builders.

Continuing the arboreal theme, these three vehicles have one other detail item of bodywork in common - all are forward entrance.

The little Renault dates back to a period when coaching optimists rather than accountants bought and ran vehicles. During the 1920s there was a vogue for small, light, continental vehicles together with American imports like the Reo. Bodywork is by Reynolds Brothers, Barnsley, one of a number of builder/operators who found a 'niche' market. Speed, incidentally, was legally limited to 12 mph, but rarely observed.

Almost archaic in appearance the 20-seater bodywork on this Commer Centurion was by Waveney and is a glorious coach-in-miniature, which any small operator would have been happy to own at the beginning of the decade but which by 1934, despite it's 6 cylinder 22.6 h.p. engine was sadly outclassed, the model only remaining in production for a year.

The chassis of this Willowbrook bodied coach was one of the finest of Leylands heavy-duty models, the Lion LT8. Both oil and petrol engines were offered and the gearbox, similar to that of the Tiger, was of the famous 'silent third' design.

With a weight only a few pounds short of six tons it's sturdiness matched the style of the body, which when built late in 1938, still had echoes of the 'Odeon' school of coach architecture but without the excessive trim often found in early postwar designs.

Each coachbuilder had their own ideas on what represented the perfect shape. Sometimes, like Mann Egerton, they tried to adapt a not unpleasant line to a most unsuitable vehicle; elsewhere, like the Burlingham Seagull body, the purity of the original was debased later. EDV 505D has a Bristol MW chassis, with an Eastern Coach Works 39-seater body. Built 1966, since then both chassis and body builders have vanished. DPR 518 has a 1949 Seddon chassis, with bodywork by an almost forgotten make, Santus of Wigan. MMR 553 belies her years in 1989. Leyland (now DAF) Tiger Cub chassis, and unusual bodywork by Harrington. 643 HAA is a pretty little 16-seat dumpling, with a modified Bedford tipper lorry chassis clothed by Plaxtons in 1963. SJW 515 is an original Burlingham Seagull body on, unusually, a Guy Arab chassis. Once a demonstrator this little gem remains in service with Dodds of Troon.

The 'innards' of the machines they travel on or in have always had a fascination for some men and a few women (otherwise why prod at the thoroughly inoffensive engine of a car every Sunday?) and seriously, it does no harm to see what is, or was, underneath the coach body.   Four drawings from the 1920s.

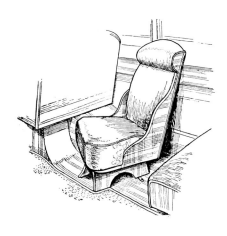

Slightly staggered seats are a feature of the latest L.M.S. coach bodies. This body was built by Watson & Son, of Lowestoft.

Single seats inclined slightly forward on a Commer coach.

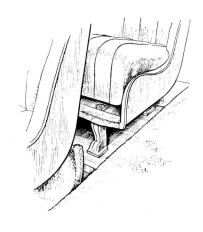

The type of armchair seat fitted by Duple Bodies to a Star coach.

The seats on one of the Metcalfe bodies are secured by four bolts that can be reached after lifting up the cushion. Fibre mats are let into the floor.

And two photographs of a 1960s Plaxton body interior.

These photographs of interiors have been deliberately chosen to illustrate different approaches to seating and finish. It was quite uneconomic for a coachbuilder to have models on hand of each of his designs, so sometimes a full-size dummy or 'buck' was utilized, where seats, racks and lighting could be swopped about. Another approach was for the company photographer to produce on film vehicles that never existed in the flesh. To compound the problems there were and to a limited extent still are, three different types of layout. The pure bus required maximum capacity, grab rails, seat bars or knobs and basic 'vandal-proof' interior fittings and materials. An express semi-coach or dual purpose vehicle needs a higher degree of trim, middle height seats, shrouded lights and some provision for luggage. A touring coach needs luxury and good baggage storage. In general bus body builders tended to make a 'pig's ear' of their coaching efforts, but conversely when coach builders essayed producing double deck bus bodies they had problems with weight, flexing and passing the tilt test.

Charles H. Roe of Leeds body appears, at first sight, to be quite sumptious but despite the table it could never be rated better than dual purpose. Longitudinal seating was never acceptable for long haul work and there is a bleakness about the interior that contrasts with the luxury of the Plaxton offering. Here we have a heater, chrome in profusion, a sliding roof, curtains, mirrors, clock and curiously prominently a fire extinguisher.

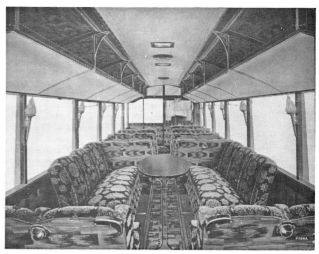

INTERIOR VIEW OF 30 SEATER SUN SALOON

The Eastern Coach Works variant falls between the two. The seats look comfortable, the floor is carpeted, there is a sun roof and quite respectable light fittings but much less trim than has the Plaxton's body, and no curtains.

Two vehicles from the same batch are shown in differing circumstances. The chassis of 223 (above) and 225 (below) were both built by the Gloucester Carriage & Wagon Company Limited whose premises were until recently among the largest in that city. Completed in 1933 these were superbly engineered machines and achieved an enviable reputation not only for reliability but for economy, at the expense it must be added of some vibration from their solidly bolted-down Gardner LW6 diesel engines. 223 is seen when brand new outside the works, 225 is at the rear of what was once the largest (and busiest) coaching interchange station in Britain, Cheltenham. Bodywork by the Gloucester company was quite remarkably luxurious, and the interior represented all that was finest in coach building at the time. Structurally they were not too sound and, surprisingly, this series of vehicles had to be rebodied by Duple in 1938, at least one example then surviving until 1956 or possibly later.

The Dennis G.L. Type.

The fear of the dreaded 'side slip' was to remain with drivers and reviewers alike for many a year; vehicles of this pattern had a relatively narrow track and an, to our eyes, enormous overhang. Given brakes only on the rear axle, solid tyres and cobbles small wonder sometimes the back wandered off on its' own, indeed a writer in 1903 stated categorically, "The only safeguard against side-slipping is to travel slowly, at a steady uniform pace. A sudden, violent application of the brake or a very strong impulse from the engine may set up slipping. The driver should, therefore, try to run his engine at an absolutely uniform speed, and should avoid travelling at a pace which would necessitate a strong application of the brake, should an obstruction suddenly block the highway [road surfaces could be deceptive]. The driver finds that he can maintain fast pace without any sign of side-slip, but he is almost helpless should the need arise for a sudden stop. If he puts the brake on suddenly the car will swing right round. A curve also will have the same affect, or an attempt to take a corner quickly." Strange to find the problem still vexing reviewers 26 years later.

"On the return journey the efficiency of the brakes was tested, and it was found that when travelling at 30 m.p.h. on a slight down gradient the vehicle could be pulled up in thirty yards with both brakes applied. Although the road was some-what slippery, not the slightest sign of side-slipping was noticeable, and I was very favourably impressed with the smooth retarding action pro-duced.

During a run in the first F type saloon coach supplied to the Westminster Coaching Services Ltd., I was able fully to appreciate the exceptionally smooth and vibrationless running of the engine; I could feel no vibration at any part of the body when the engine was raced with the clutch disen-gaged, and practically the only noise was that caused by suction of the carburetter."

Dennis F Type specification.

MAIN DETAILS AND DIMENSIONS

Engine.
 Cylinders : Four, en bloc, two-piece detachable head.
  Bore : 110 mm. (4$\frac{5}{16}$in.).
  Stroke : 150 mm. (5$\frac{15}{16}$in.).
  Capacity : 5,702 c.c.
  Horse-power : 30. R.A.C. rating, 47 b.h.p. at 1,000 r.p m. ; 64 b.h.p. at 1,500 r.p.m.
 Cooling System : Impeller pump, gilled tube radiator and belt-driven fan.
 Carburation : Claudel-Hobson, hot-water jacketed and " hot-spot."
 Lubrication : Forced by gear pump through camshaft to cam-shaft and crankshaft bearings.
 Ignition : High-tension magneto, variable timing.

Transmission.
 Clutch : Fabric-faced cone with two adjustable clutch stops.
 Gear Box : Separate, driven by flexible disc jointed shaft. Four forward and reverse speeds. Right-hand control.
 Propeller-Shaft : One-piece, tubular with Hook type universal joints.
 Back Axle : Under-driving worm and full-floating shafts to wheel hubs.

Road Wheels.
 Detachable pressed-steel disc pattern.

Tyres.
 Straight-sided pneumatic, 36×6in. (38×7in. at extra charge), single front, twin rear.

Brakes.
 Pedal, expanding in front and rear wheel drums, servo-assisted.
 Hand, expanding in independent drums on rear wheels.

Springs.
 Front, semi-elliptic above axle.
 Rear, semi-elliptic below axle.

Steering.
 Worm and sector.

General Dimensions.
 Wheelbase : 16ft. 7$\frac{1}{2}$in.
 Track : Front, 5ft. 11in. Rear, 5ft. 6in.
 Overall Length : 25ft. 10$\frac{1}{8}$in.
 Overall Width : 7ft. 2in.
 Dashboard to Rear End of Frame : 20ft. 10$\frac{3}{4}$in.
 Centre of Back Axle to Rear End of Frame : 6ft. 9$\frac{3}{4}$in.
 Height of Frame (Loaded) : 25in. to 26in.
 Ground Clearance up to Back Axle : 10$\frac{1}{2}$in.
 Ground Clearance under Back Axle : 7in.
 Turning Circle Diameter : 60ft. (approx.).
 Chassis Weight : 3 tons (approx.).
 Load Capacity : Up to 30 passengers.
 Chassis Price : £885.

When this Duple advertisement first appeared in 1946 no-one really knew what shape the coach of the future would take. Delivery, too, was restricted by a Government policy of 'Export or Die' with the result that the home market was starved of vehicles and delivery, once promised as 16 weeks, slid back to as many months. In the meantime, however, you could buy a Bedford OB between 1945 and 1951; including a few made pre-war, 12766 were manufactured. Not surprisingly 200 or more remain today and in one 'proper' coaching can still be enjoyed.

"Hey, look!

What a super coach! I wish I could have a ride in it!" Of course he does, bless him. Even at his age he can appreciate the beautiful lines of Duple Coachwork. What he *can't* appreciate is the wealth of craftsmanship—the brilliant combination of design with construction—that has gone into its evolution. But he will—one day—because he's going to be a big transport manager, like his uncle, running a *whole fleet* of "super coaches." And what's more, he'll see that they all have Duple bodywork.

DUPLE BODIES & MOTORS LIMITED, HENDON, LONDON

Our honeymoon couple having first selected the coach style they like must necessarily make their way to the coach station to see what services are on offer. And coach stations vary enormously in size from a garage - or even indeed the operator's yard, to a massive modern structure echoing the best in architecture. But, alas, more often than not coach stations were and are the Achilles Heel of the whole concern, for the conditions underfoot all too often left much to be desired. Our couple turn up for the 6 a.m. departure. The sparrows cough, the garage is still gloomy with the lifeless coaches lined up, their dulled bedewed chrome trim giving a mastodon-like effect. Somewhere a pipe drips, somewhere someone sneezes.

Travel Wisely and Well
by COACH

Information and tickets from local agents

Over eight million people pass through Victoria Coach Station every year using the fast regular coach services operating daily to all parts of Britain. Every passenger has a guaranteed seat at no extra cost. Connections are made at sea-ports and air-ports for overseas travel to the continent, Ireland, Isle of Wight, Channel Islands, Scilly Isles and the Isle of Man.

LONDON COASTAL COACHES LTD
VICTORIA COACH STATION
LONDON S.W.1

One advantage coaches have always had over the railway is that a seat is guaranteed, wisely this 1963 advertisement stresses the fact.

Vaguely one hears a mechanic tish as he drops a spanner in a pool of indescribable sludge. Oil, water and exhaust fumes permeate the very structure. The Inspector has that waxen skin of a night shift man and with the best will in the world cannot avoid sounding dull and depressed. The cafeteria remains firmly closed and the 2d chocolate machine has long since ceased to disgorge its bars. Wasn't it like this? Not always, sometimes the wind howled through the canyons and made it worse!

London Coastal Coaches ended up at the latest and probably finest coach station in London. Opened in March 1932 most major companies eventually ended up being based there; seen when new a Royal Blue coach sits outside, ready to load.

Coach Station Contrasts

Burnells Garage, Knightstone Road, Weston-super-Mare in the late 1920s. The rather pleasant building next door to the yard was the Glentworth Hall Hotel, subsequently demolished.

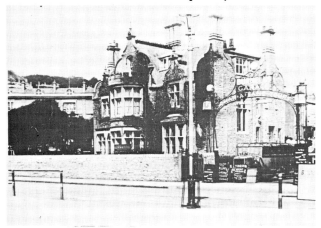

Burnell's Garage - Late 1920s.

Haymarket Bus Station, Newcastle, seen in 1966. The destinations prove the word 'bus' to be a misnomer and some say the Burlingham Seagull bodied Leyland of Camplejohn Bros. (of Barnsley, Yorkshire) represented the peak of coach design. Interesting, too, are the ancillary activities of the area with a cafe, snack bar, and Tatler Cartoon Cinema vying for your custom. The cartoon cinema was once a feature to be found near bus depots and railway stations with a continuous programme of cartoons running - an hour was generally sufficient to see them all, but no-one threw you out!

Haymarket Bus Station 1966

The Croydon Coaching Centre reflected both the importance of coach work (whether day trips or tours) in a predominantly middle-class area. Their coach station was quite orthodox whereas Birch Brothers' represented the height of 'Odeon' architecture, even down to the Cafe Airflo. After its opening in 1937 the building must have been most reassuring to would-be customers travelling from or arriving at Rushden.

Vine Street Bus Station, Scarborough, often housed a number of interesting vehicles. Notable among other details is the predominance of 'bible' blinds, solid, hinged boards replacing the more orthodox cloth ones used elsewhere. Visible are three 1935 Dennis Lancets, and a 1937 Bristol J of West Yorkshire plus a Leyland Tiger TS7 with, interestingly, 'East Yorks' cast in the radiator header tank trim.

Cafe Airflo and Birch Brothers

Vine Street Bus Station

IN presenting this booklet for your perusal we would respectfully draw your attention to the fact that we act as agents only. We are official agents for every first class service, without exception, operating anywhere in England, Scotland and Wales including the London Coastal Coaches, Ltd. We are the only road travel firm in this district with this distinction. We are thus in the unique position of being able to offer absolutely unbiassed advice. Please do not hesitate to ask for information, be it only about a 1/- journey on the Green Line. You are assured of civility and a keen desire to help. It is because we have taken pains with every enquiry, however small, that we have now one of the largest Road Travel Booking Offices in London, enjoying the confidence both of the public and operators. All services mentioned in this booklet are thoroughly reliable, if therefore, we appear to " push " any particular service it is only because of the continued recommendation of experienced travellers. We guarantee that all coaches are modern with centre gangways and, invariably, armchair seating. The majority of vehicles are periodically inspected by the police, the drivers being picked men holding Scotland Yard driving licenses. In some cases the long distance coaches do not start from Croydon. For the convenience of passengers we have a fleet of modern cars which pick up anywhere in this district at slight additional cost. Travellers by road can thus get from Croydon to anywhere in luxury, at a cost which bears favourable comparison with the cheapest excursion fares.

Had our honeymoon couple lived in the 1920s one would hope the husband was able to keep his employment and that they would be able to enjoy their days out in a char-a-banc before the almost inevitable family came along.

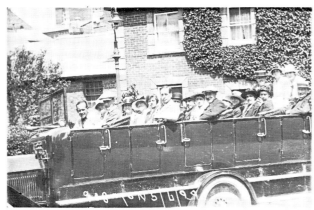

A perfectly ordinary outing photograph can conceal an interesting story. This group were the bell ringers of Eastwell Parish near Ashford in Kent. The population was 897 and 18 of them including the Parson went to Margate for their annual do.

Were there honeymoon couples among this 1922 departure? One likes to think so.

Here we have a coaching mystery. Presumably this is an outing (the coach is based at Brighton) although the vehicle could have been commandeered for use by Territorials; the passengers are (nearly) all Sergeants of one sort or another, although the driver is a civilian. Who are the girls? There have been many unusual coaching stories, surely this is another.

The scenario is of a smallish town with a working railway albeit one that caters only for business men going to and from town plus a market train. No evening services nor Sundays. Fred, the greengrocer, cannot afford to run a coach but there is a demand for darts-night outings and the like. Fred's solution? Take off his lorry body and fit £15 worth of chara body as required, a bus-o-lorry as it were.

The Gorge at Cheddar, while famous for it's high, steep sides, with a road so narrow that two charabancs could not pass was also imfamous for falling rocks - a notice warned of the danger. In modern times although access has been improved and the scenery is still spectacular some coach operators are reluctant to drive up the gorge from the village and caves, disembarking their passengers at the lower level. In the summertime strawberry teas are still available which was, no doubt, one of the delights our passengers here, starting from Weston-super-Mare sea-front, were anticipating.

Each generation thinks that it is quite unique and rarely can children visualize that their parents might have had the same pleasures, wishes and ambitions as they. "Did you really go to the seaside?" was a question I once asked my father. So our honeymoon couple might have asked theirs and out came the old postcards to prove it.

1911: "Motor-omnibuses are still to a certain extent in the experimental stage, since no-one would suggest that they have yet attained to the greatest possible perfection, while further improvements in them are constantly being announced. Yet already their number has enormously increased...".

Public service vehicles reached their peak, numerically, in 1952 with 41,000 single deckers of all types registered. Within seven years the bubble burst and numbers fell to 36,000 never again to rise.

SAMUELSON

SAMUELSON

"Pride of the Moor" belonged to a Plymouth operator. The 8th of June 1922 outing, below left, was to an unknown "Crab & Lobster" while visitors - all ladies - to Sandown, the Isle of Wight, toured gently in Moss Motor Tours vehicle at 20mph.

The generation game (top to bottom) charabancs 1910, Paignton, a Crossley loading at Nottingham for Yarmouth in the early 1930s and happy trippers at Margate twenty years later.

The real winter for coaching came in the 1930s when many firms, with little reserves of cash, found their vehicles, bought with such ease a decade before, to be finally failing and outdated. Cash for new was not forthcoming, but with the incurable optimism that is necessary for all private coach proprietors, hire purchase agreements were entered into. Alas, there were no longer the passengers to pay for these luxurious vehicles and additionally there are too many stories about the ruthlessness of h.p concerns for them not to be true - a favourite was to wait for the vehicles payment to be due on the Sunday. Human nature demands that this should be paid on the Monday but exactly at midnight a roar would indicate a snatch-back. "Heavies" prevented any redress and the law, inevitably, was on the side of the money-lender. One week's reporting reprinted from Motor Transport, January 12th, 1931, will suffice to show how hard the winter was.

FINANCIAL NEWS

COUNTY COURT JUDGMENTS

The following returns, received from the Registry of County Court Judgments, House of Lords, purport to contain judgments entered up in the respective county courts of England and Wales. No distinction is made on the register between actions for debts or damages or properly disputed cases; neither is it known which of the judgments remain unpaid at the present time. A large proportion of judgments may have been settled between the parties or paid. The name given is that of the defendants; the amount is that for which judgment was given, and the date is that on which it was given.

— **Armstrong,** 136, Front Street, West Auckland, Durham, haulage contractor; court, Bishop Auckland, £10 1s. 10d. Dec. 5.

C. E. Billington, Railway Junction Inn, Nightingale Road, Hitchin, Herts, bus proprietor; court, West London (Brompton), £10 6s. 6d. Dec. 8.

R. Blacow, 52, Ellworth Street, Sandbach, Ches, haulage contractor; court, Warrington, £29 15s. 6d. Dec. 11.

G. B. Blenkinsop, 121, Alliance Avenue, Hull, haulage contractor; court, Kingston-upon-Hull, £19 7s. 8d. Dec. 11.

E. T. Bridges, 214, Brockley Road, Brockley, S.E., contractor; court, Greenwich, £22 7s. Dec. 5.

M. V. Burnett, Hemingby, Lincs, haulage contractor; court, Great Grimsby, £10 2s. 8d. Nov. 27.

Thos. Bywater(s), 32, Sneinton Hermitage, Nottingham, haulage contractor; court, Nottingham, £52 13s. 4d. Dec. 11.

W. Cockerill (trading as Cockerill & Grimshaw), Oak Avenue, Rising Bridge, Haslingden, Lancs, haulage contractor; court, Accrington, £39 15s. 6d. Dec. 10.

R. A. Dagnall, Hales Place, Canterbury, haulage contractor; court, Canterbury, £149 13s. 6d. Dec. 2.

M. Farnorth & Sons (a firm), Hanson Street, Middleton, Lancs, haulage contractors; court, Liverpool, £38 14s. 10d. Nov. 27.

T. Fazackerley, 74, Mill Street, Farington, near Preston, haulage contractor; court, Preston, £26 9s. 9d. Dec. 9.

C. B. Fowler, No. 6 Flat, Devon House, Kings Down Parade, Bristol, haulage contractor; court, Westminster, £106 18s. 10d. Nov. 28.

H. C. France (Carriers), Ltd., 64b, Banning Street, Greenwich, S.E., carriers; court, Greenwich, £22 5s. 10d. Dec. 3.

A. Hessle (trading as Wilberfoss Haulage Co.), Wilberfoss, Yorks, haulage contractor; court, York, £16 8s. 8d. Dec. 4.

P. High, 7, Corporation Road, Wisbech, Cambs, bus proprietor; court, Great Grimsby, £14 4s. Dec. 9.

J. Kennedy, 83, George Street, Mansfield, Notts, haulage contractor; court, Mansfield, £28 8s. 6d. Dec. 8.

J. H. Kitchener, 18, Cross Street, St. Annes-on-Sea, Lancs, coach proprietor; court, Blackpool, £12 14s. 1d. Dec. 9.

W. Levy, 68, Blackwall Lane, Greenwich, Kent, bus proprietor; court, Maidstone, £10 19s. 3d. Nov. 25.

Longton Bros. (a firm), 2, Bridge Street, Whittle-le-Woods, Chorley, Lancs, coach proprietors; court, Southport and Ormskirk, £15 17s. Dec. 5.

G. W. Marsden, 38, Euston Road, Morecambe, Lancs, haulage contractor; court, Lancaster, £14 10s. 7d. Dec. 11.

Martin Transport Co. (a firm), 46, Fenwick Street, Liverpool, contractors; court, Newcastle-under-Lyme, £13 0s. 3d. Dec. 8.

J. Milner, Kepwick House, Rowlands Gill, Durham, haulage contractor; court, North Shields, £22 5s. Dec. 5.

W. Nettleton, 54, St. James Street, Wetherby, York, haulage contractor; court, Leeds, £19 8s. 6d. Nov. 26.

Eleanor Annie Nobbs (trading as Regent Coaches), Kent Square, Great Yarmouth, Norfolk; court, Bloomsbury, £14 17s. 4d. Nov. 20.

J. W. Pedlingham, 532, Green Lane, Small Heath, Birmingham, haulage contractor; court, Bloomsbury, £10 18s. 2d. Dec. 5.

Ryder & Ashcroft (a firm), 3, Green Lane, Hindley Green, Hindley, Lancs, haulage contractors; court, Wigan, £19 4s. 6d. Dec. 4.

John Smith, The Bungalow, The Moor, Bilsthorpe, Nottingham, haulage contractor; court, West Bromwich, £21 18s. 6d. Nov. 25.

Southern Services (Cardiff), Ltd., Motor House, Wood Street, Cardiff, travel agents; court, Cardiff, £10 12s. 6d. Dec. 4.

Stanley Bros. (a firm), 100, Junction Road, Andover, Hants, bus proprietors; court, Edmonton and Wood Green, £21 5s. 9d. Oct. 27.

Stepney Haulage, Ltd., 209, Barnardo Street, Stepney, E., haulage contractors; court, West London (Brompton), £14 15s. 1d. Dec. 9.

W. R. Swinn, 3, Commercial Road, Bulwell, Notts, transport contractor; court, Nottingham, £10 1s. 6d. Dec. 10.

A. Ward, 43, Thornes Lane, Wakefield, Yorks, haulage contractor; court, Wakefield, £30 14s. 4d. Dec. 9.

J. S. Weston, Church Aston, Newport, Salop, haulier; court, Wellington, Salop, £10 3s. 8d. Dec. 4.

E. Westwood, 28, Highfield Crescent, Highfield Road, Blackheath, Staffs, haulage contractor; court, West Bromwich, £17 10s. 11d. Nov. 26.

THE GAZETTE

It is pointed out that winding-up proceedings and liquidations are frequently rendered necessary for the purpose of reconstruction, extension of capital, transfer of business, etc., quite unconnected with any financial embarrassment, and the fact that companies appear in this list, therefore, must not of necessity be taken as indicating any want of solvency. There is nothing in the ordinary official notification to show whether the case is one of formal winding-up for administration purposes or not.

Douglas Bros. (E. Douglas, 44, Springfield Terrace, Bailiffe Bridge, near Brighouse, Yorks, and G. Douglas, 91, Smith House Estate, Brighouse, trading as), haulage contractors, 44, Springfield Terrace, Bailiffe Bridge, near Brighouse.—Receiving order December 23, 1930.

A. C. McNab, haulage contractor, 81, Mayband Avenue, Sudbury, late of 14, Buckingham Road, Edgware.—Receiving order December 22, 1930.

E. T. Mills, farmer and haulage contractor, "Melrose," Great Oakley, Harwich, Essex.—Public examination February 5, 1931, at Law Courts, Town Hall, Colchester.

J. J. Lister, coach proprietor, 290, Shirley Road, Southampton.—Receiving order December 30, 1930.

T. Halliday, jun., haulage contractor, 26, Cowling Road, Windhill, Shipley, late of 9, Ives Street, Shipley, Yorks.—Public examination February 13, 1931, at The County Court, Manor Row, Bradford.

Elizabeth Whinn, late bus proprietress, 17, Highfield Villas, York Road, Sherburn-in-Elmet, Yorks.—Public examination January 16, 1931, at Court House, Raglan Street, Harrogate.

E. J. Hills, haulier, 1, Primrose Cottage, Victoria Road, Upper Parkstone, Dorset.—First meeting January 14, 1931, at the Law Courts, Stafford Road, Bournemouth. Public examination February 6, 1931, at The Law Courts, Stafford Road, Bournemouth.

PARTNERSHIP DISSOLVED

Burchall & Co., haulage contractors and garage proprietors, Hertford Road, Freezywater, Waltham Cross, Herts.—Dissolution of partnership between J. J. Burchall and W. J. Collins. Debts settled by J. J. Burchall, who continues under the same style.

BANKRUPTCY PROCEEDINGS

London & Counties Carriage Co., Ltd., 50-51, High Holborn, London, W.C.—In the compulsory liquidation of this company, the registered office of which was formerly at 49a, George Street, Croydon, the statutory meetings of the creditors and shareholders were held at the Board of Trade Offices, 33, Carey Street, W.C. The winding-up order was made on November 24 on a creditor's petition. The company was incorporated in June, 1928, with a nominal capital of £1,000 to carry on the business of motor coach proprietors, etc., and the capital issued was £750. Owing to trouble with vehicles which frequently broke down, the company's regular services were not maintained, and it was unable to pay the instalments due under hire-purchase agreements. As a result of the meetings the liquidation remained in the hands of the Official Receiver. No statement of affairs has yet been filed.

Safeways (a firm), 87, Bounds Green Road, London, N.22.—Lack of capital and competition by another coach service with which he was unable to compete, were the causes of failure attributed by this debtor, R. W. Priest. The receiving order was made against him on a creditor's petition in October last, and he had lodged a statement of affairs showing liabilities of £2,180 17s. 3d. against assets of £60 15s. 5d. In June, 1927, with £400 capital, debtor commenced trading as a coach proprietor, obtaining on hire-purchase a coach for £1,400. In November, 1927, he started a service from London to Luton, which later was extended to Bedford. Other coaches were obtained on the hire-purchase system and the first-mentioned was sold for £850. He sold the goodwill of the business in March, 1929, also the interest in four coaches, for £3,000, and after payment of his liabilities he had a balance of £2,200. In May, 1929, with that amount as capital, he commenced a further business at Wood Green, again as a coach proprietor, under the unregistered name of Safeways Coaches. A service from London to Reading was commenced and was successful. In July, 1929, a limited company was promoted to take over the business, the nominal capital to be £200, divided into 400 shares of 10s. each. No shares were issued and the company never operated. In October another private concern commenced a service on the same route, and through lack of capital the debtor was unable to compete successfully. In July, 1930, the owners of the coaches he had acquired on the hire-purchase system, obtained judgment against him, taking possession of the three vehicles. As a result of the first meeting of creditors the Official Receiver remained trustee.

COMPANY RESULTS AND NOTICES

United Service Transport Co., Ltd.—The accounts of this company for the year ended September 30, 1930, show a profit of £29,936 (£43,141). After providing £22,051 (£32,203) for depreciation, the net profit was £7,885 (£10,938). After providing for the preference dividend it is proposed to pay a dividend of 8 per cent. (the same) on the ordinary shares, leaving £181 (£159 last year, when £3,000 was added to reserve) to be carried forward.

Sternol, Ltd.—The directors of this company announce that the preliminary figures show insufficient margin to cover the second half-year's preference dividend, and it was therefore decided not to pay a further dividend on December 31, 1930.

Hoyal Body Corporation (1928), Ltd.—A trading loss of £4,800 is shown in the accounts for the thirteen months ended August 31, 1930, of this company. In the previous period there was a loss of £5,834.

NEW COMPANIES

Colin Haines, Ltd.—Capital £1,000. To manufacture, export, import and deal in private and commercial motors and other vehicles, etc. First and permanent managing director: C. Haines. Solicitor, E. Marchant, Bletchley. Private company.

London & East Coast Motors, Ltd.—Capital £200. To carry on the business of and dealers in motor cars, bus proprietors and carriers of passengers and goods, etc. Directors: W. A. Kay and S. G. Suffill. Registered office: 17, High Ousegate, York. Private company.

RECEIVERSHIP (APPOINTMENT OR RELEASE)

Low Loaders, Ltd.—Mr. B. Davis, of Sceptre House, 169, Regent Street, W., was appointed receiver and manager on December 30, 1930, under powers contained in debenture dated September 27, 1930.

Second-hand Motor Coaches and Buses for Sale.

One penny per word: minimum 1/-.

A.J.S.

A.J.S. 26-seater Saloon, coachwork by Lewis and Crabtree, upholstered moquette, small mileage, perfect every way, this coach and also a 26-seater Lioness must be sold, and low prices will be taken.—Hodgson, 174, North Rd., Preston.   [1628

Bean.

1930 Bean All-weather, Scotland Yard type, 16-17-seater coach, fitted 4 wheel brakes and numerous extras, chassis and body in perfect condition; £410; any reasonable trial arranged.—Pass and Joyce, Ltd., Commercial Vehicle Department, 373-375, Euston Rd., N.W.1. Tel.: Museum 8401. T.A.: Bestocars, London.   [1669

Chevrolet.

14-SEATER Domed Back Saloon Coach on Chevrolet; £150 for quick sale.
20-SEATER 6-wheeler Chevrolet Bus, reconditioned; £175.
20-SEATER Service Bus on W. and G., perfect, guaranteed; £300.
14-SEATER Chevrolet Bus, in excellent condition throughout; £85.
R.E.A.L. CARRIAGE WORKS, Ltd., Popes Lane, Ealing. 'Phone: Ealing 5966.   [0229
100 Goods and Passenger Vehicles in Stock; list post free to Lancs and Yorks and all Britain; new and used Chevrolet, large and small, exchanges and terms; distance no object; write, 'phone or call.—Bambers, Birkdale, Southport. 'Phone: Birkdale 66161.   [8742

De Dion.

DE DION, about 1925, 20-seater charabanc, disc wheels and spare, good pneumatic tyres all round, twins on rear; accept £45, or near offer.—Tucker, Alperton Lodge, Ealing Rd., Alperton. Wembley 2694.   [1460

Dennis.

FOR Sale, 3 26-seater all-weather Dennis motor coaches, also one 14-seater all-weather Dennis motor coach; no reasonable offer refused.—Apply Symes and Sons, Ltd., Terrace Rd., Bournemouth.   [1070

Du Cros.

DU CROS.
20- and 26-seater Second-hand Coaches, in good order, for immediate delivery.—Apply W. and G. Du Cros, Ltd., 177, The Vale, Acton, W.3.   [0438

Lancia.

LANCIA 1928 26-seater All-weather Coach, dome back, leather upholstery, in excellent condition; £550.—Blaxton's, 112, Belvedere Rd., S.E.1.   Hop 3115.   [8454

Overland.

1925 Overland Saloon 'Bus, pneumatic tyres on all wheels 2 spares, dynamo lighting and starting, in excellent condition throughout; £22/10.—Tucker, Alperton Lodge, Ealing Rd., Alperton. Wembley 2694.   [1459

Reo.

REO 1928 (late) 20-seater Coach, fine order, splendid body; £195.—Globe Auto Service, Vicarage Rd., Hampton Wick, Middlesex.   [0494

Saurer.

SAURER Type 2 B.H. 'Bus, complete with 20-seater front entrance body and rear emergency door, 32×6 single and twin tyres, year of manufacture September, 1928, perfect running order and good condition
SAURER Type 2 B.H. 'Bus, complete with 20-seater front entrance body and rear emergency door, fitted with 32×6 single and twin tyres, year of manufacture early 1929, perfect running order and good condition.—Oswald Tillotson (1929), Ltd., New Preston St., Bradford. 'Phone: 8174.   [0466

Studebaker.

£14/10, or near offer.—10-seater Studebaker charabanc, first class running order, nearly new tyres, lighting and starting; must sell.—Tucker, Alperton Lodge, Ealing Rd., Alperton. Wembley 2694.   [1461

It took a brave man to buy any of these, and the guarantee given between the wars was probably worth no more than the one Sid gave you from his bomb-site. The fascination lies in the makes. 'Scotland Yard type' for the Bean meant that it met the requirements of the Metropolitan Police who licensed vehicles for use in London, not that it was normally used by men with pipes and trench raincoats!

In Commercial Motor of 31 May 1932 these drawings accompanied a scholarly dissertation on the structure and weatherproofing requirements of a coach or bus roof. The problems were manifold not the least being that only a few years separated this charabanc with its rubberised canvas and "today's [1932] most modern" design. Sliding roof sections were still obligatory (indeed it took until the 1960s for these to disappear) and for long distance work baggage was still loaded on the roof and covered by an (almost) waterproof cover.

Maintenance gave problems. In 1950 the Duple manual required: *At each corner of the sliding roof will be found a small hole, which is the outlet for a length of hose which carries water away. This tube must be kept clear of dirt and leaves, or it will become clogged and water will accumulate and lead to deterioration and roof leaks.*

At least once a week a thin cane should be passed through the holes both ways. Wire should never be used, as it will damage the tubing.

Sliding hatches in the roof of a Davidson body.

Making Adequate Provision for the Carriage of Luggage. Current Designs of Roof and How They are Constructed

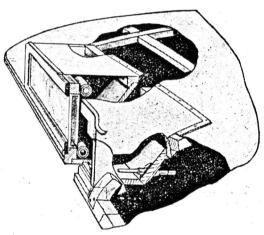

(Above) A part-sectional view of a front destination indicator that is built into the roof.

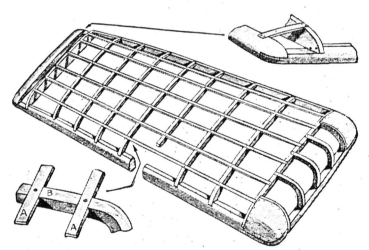

(Left) The roof framework for a small coach; it is intended to be covered with a flexible material, so as to form a non-drumming structure. One of the detail drawings shows a section of the front framework and the other the method of lapping lengthwise battens A and roofstick B.

(Right) The left part of this drawing shows a roof with its inside panelling and the method of fixing the lamp (A) and the ventilator (B), the other part showing the framework. A section through the front ventilator is shown at C.

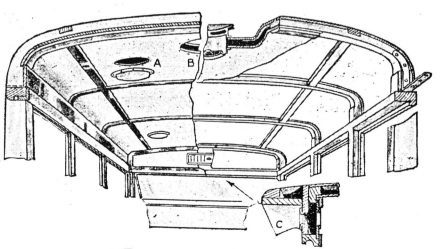

Royal Blue RU 8807 was an AEC Reliance brought into service 11 April 1929. In 1935 this coach passed to Southern National, whose number 3712 is on the bonnet side, by which time the original all-weather, Duple body, was outdated, a new Beadle of Dartford saloon being fitted to the chassis in 1936. The vehicle was sold in 1948.

In this photograph, taken at Cheltenham, behind is an original Elliott Bros. (pre-Royal Blue) coach, distinguished by the anti-scuff ribs on the side.

This Weymann bodied AEC for Midland General was the pride of the fleet when new just four years after the article appeared. Many years later a coachbuilding company saw the answer to roof leaks to lie in fibreglass, but seepage between the sections cost them a hard earned reputation and contributed to their disappearance.

Most body builders advertisements appeared in trade magazines where they would, hopefully, catch the eye of transport managers and members of local council transport committees (although it was always doubted if they had the ability to read, let alone the desire) but an alternative was the use of 'freebie' postcards. London Lorries issued a few in the 1930s, although reproducable ones are as rare as hens' teeth, and the real vogue came in the 1950s. Oddly Beccols showed a coach without their 'trademark' - a sort of Widow's Peak arrangement, but Burlingham got it right.

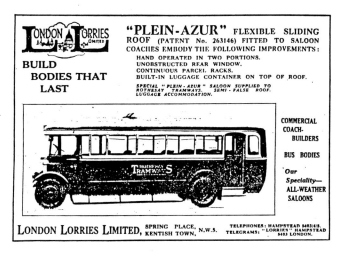

'SEAGULL' SUPER LUXURY COACH
by
H. V. BURLINGHAM LTD., Preston New Road, BLACKPOOL.   Phone : Marton 251

33 SEATER LUXURY COACH

By BECCOLS LTD.
Phone : Westhoughton 2222

Chequerbent, Bolton, Lancashire
Grams : Coachwork, Westhoughton

Fanfare

FOR ALL OPERATORS

◄ *The Fanfare* has a clean spacious interior of modern design with wide, well padded luggage racks. Seating 37 to 41 passengers it is easily convertible for use as a bus if required.

◄ *The driver's compartment* is provided with a waist-high partition with door and curved screen and curtain behind the driver. Anti-glare shields are fitted to the curved roof panels.

Careful design is evinced by the inward opening door with flush handrail and handle. There is a transparent panel in the door at step level and the step lamp is automatically operated. ►

METROPOLITAN · CAMMELL · WEYMANN LIMITED

VICKERS HOUSE, WESTMINSTER, LONDON, S.W.1.

This letter, ostensibly from Mrs. Bailey, appeared in Passenger Transport, 16 December 1953, but a lady colleague of mine has very grave doubts whether it was a woman who wrote it. Be that as it may in 1954 there were available around 1,500 shades of colour in coachpaint (there are still 300-plus) but what could, or can, beat the simplicity of Black & White Coachways' layout or the two greens and cream of West Riding, London Transport's real red, Royal Blue's blue, or any of the smart two-tone OBs operated by village operators. It was both the quality of the original (5 or 6 coats was normal), and the cleanliness that marked a good vehicle. What would Mrs. Bailey have thought of National Grubby White, Poppy Pink, or Publican's Green that we had until recently, let alone the too-often tawdry finishes (one coat sprayed on irregardless of base colour) we see today?

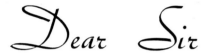

THE WOMAN'S POINT OF VIEW

Sir,—For too long have so many of my sex put up with so little imagination in the choice of the tedious designs and uninteresting colour combinations in passenger transport.

Mere Man will probably admit the comforts from a Woman's "touch" in the home, particularly from those with taste and imagination, also colour sense. I wonder how long it will be before transport interests will bring into consultation the Woman's point of view?

I am only too aware of the economics in having designs suitable for cutting, etc., but my complaint is based on the apparent lack of originality, the drabness in colour contrast and fear of trying something quite different.

To add some support to my arguments I consider Women have a natural flair for colour sense in the choice of dress and general wearing apparel, whereas the business Man with his dreary official dress cannot be expected to have colour sense, and even if he is blessed with some unusual artistic sense he is not in daily contact with colour choice and therefore cannot be expected to have that originality which I claim is so desirable.

The essence of good design is to produce something which strikes a pleasing note immediately and which one can live with without loss of interest.

I am not a fan for the contemporary designs, although some of it is good sense and original. My choice would be based upon something as natural as possible, for we live with the beauties of nature without getting tired of it, and therefore we are likely to be pleased by something based on nature and which holds an interest in shape, rather than some design which completely lacks interest or colour and which has been produced solely on the basis of cutting economy.

There is enough drabness in an everyday existence of the majority to warrant a change in official outlook to brighten our everyday travel. I believe the Woman's touch could do much to introduce colours and contrasts which would tend to liven one's daily interest rather than subdue it by the almost complete lack of design interest in transport. I say " almost," for just before leaving London I caught sight of something different on a London Underground train which I have presumed to be an experiment. If this assumption is correct, then it has tickled my interest in believing that we may expect some improvement in the near future.

Yours faithfully,
Mrs. COLIN C. BAILEY.
Ashton-on-Ribble, Preston.

Kearsleys were one of a dozen manufacturers of coach-paints at the time of the advert, and blessed with a dry sense of humour that did them well.

It is often considered to be the ultimate insult to compare someone's face with that of the back of a bus, but to tell a girl she looks like the rear of Bolton Corporation No.1 coach (Leyland TS8C/Park Royal) must be the highest accolade possible. ABN 401 was ordered as a "thirty-two single deck (special) omnibus" on the 27th of May 1938, the body alone costing £670. The vehicle was registered on the 10th of August that year. The last known owner was R & T Howarth, Rochdale, 401's licence expiring on 31st December 1961.

Leyland TS8C/Park Royal

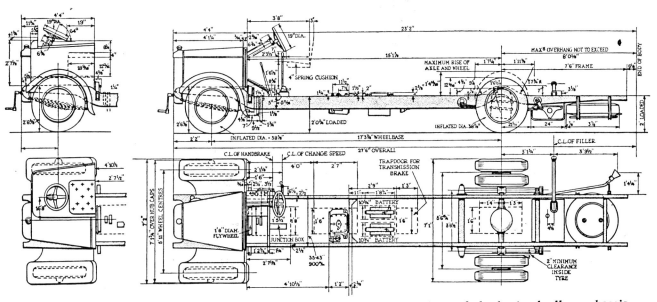

Coachbuilders' general-arrangement drawings, giving principal dimensions of the long wheelbase chassis with both normal and forward control driving positions.

Chapter Two

Inclusive Tours

If the prospect of arranging an individual trip with all the problems of arranging coaches, hotels and meals was too much why not go with an organised party? Fares were reasonable, but generally pitched high enough to keep the less affluent away, hotels were thoroughly British, and one visited most of the 'nicer' parts. And, oh yes, as Thomas Cook put it "the chauffeurs are all experienced drivers and competent mechanics". Southdown had long been in the forefront of tour operators, for someone with about ten weeks wages to spare (50 guineas = £52.50) this 1949 trip was very good value for money - a wise passenger took about the same again for tips and spending money. The biggest problem was the necessity to pack sufficient variation in clothing within the confines of one "medium-sized suitcase" - the maximum permitted. One could, however, forward extra baggage to a point en route. Hotels undertook to provide laundry facilities. In distinct contrast with the sophistication of Southdown, Epsom tours offered a pleasant amble around East Anglia at a far cheaper rate (£2.10 per night against £2.90). Both, alas, were dependant upon reasonable weather; but then the sun nearly always shone on us!

TOUR OF BRITAIN

Here is a tour which will immediately appeal to those who wish to explore the beauties and historic sites of Britain in the most convenient way and time. To overseas visitors with a limited stay in this country, affords a unique opportunity to fulfil an often expressed desire.

As the great panorama daily unfolds with ever changing beauty and charm, so famous names from the past come forward, as prompted by the specialised knowledge of the courier.

Adequate times are scheduled to permit the viewing of special points of interest, and from the abridged itinerary and route map, it will readily be seen how this tour derives its title.

TOUR No. L16

18 DAYS

*

INCLUSIVE FARE

50 guineas

*

DEPARTURES FROM

LONDON
Victoria Coach Station
(9.30 a.m.)

on each

TUESDAY
JUNE 7th to SEPTEMBER 13th

3-DAY TOUR OF EAST ANGLIA

(visiting the Royal Sandringham Estate, King's Lynn and Norfolk Broads)

Centred at the Castle Hotel, Norwich

£6. 6. 0.

First day : via Chelmsford, Colchester (stop), and Ipswich by-pass to Norwich—dinner, bed and breakfast.

Second day : via Dereham, Swaffham to King's Lynn (stop), thence Sandringham to view the Royal Estate, returning via Fakenham, Aylsham, to Norwich—dinner, bed and breakfast.

Third day : via Beccles to Oulton Broad, famous yachting centre, returning to Norwich for lunch. The return journey via Thetford, Barton Mills, Newmarket and Bishop's Stortford.

General Information. Dinner, bed and breakfast is included in the inclusive fare for the first and second nights. Lunch is also provided on the third day. Other arrangements for meals are not included, in order that each individual passenger may make the best possible use of his time. Sufficient time is given at each stop in which to obtain a meal and do a certain amount of sightseeing. Norwich has a very fine Cathedral and is an extremely interesting city. The visits to King's Lynn and Sandringham should be of great interest to all.

Departure dates : May 15, July 5, August 1 and September 5.

Departure points & times: Dorking 8.30; Ashtead 8.50; Epsom 9 a.m.

(Right) The markings on this brochure are those of the original customer.

Not many people now even remember what an identity card was; an ex-Home Guard told me that the very least penalty for not carrying it in 1941 was that you would be shot . . . Special arrangements existed for hotels to draw sufficient food, although the quality was very variable, with horse-flesh, very peculiar fish and whalemeat appearing under various guises. But at least the girls were pretty, the boys gallant and the sun always shone.

RED AND WHITE SERVICES LTD.

All-British Holiday Tours.

3 Victoria Colonnade,

Southampton Row - - W.C.I.

Telephone : HOLborn **9914**. 1937.

Dear Sir or Madam,

It is with much pleasure that we once again offer for your kind consideration a selection of fascinating Holidays by Motor Coach, both in Great Britain and the Continent.

As you will no doubt appreciate, it is impossible to cover all our Tours in this one Book but may we request that you give us the opportunity of submitting a quotation for a Tour of any duration to any part, to suit your individual requirements.

We can recommend the arrangements outlined with all certainty, but feel that perfection can only be attained by close co-operation between the Client and the Organiser, may we therefore earnestly impress upon you how glad we should be to receive your criticisms.

We should be most happy to meet you to discuss any Tour in which you may be interested, or to offer suggestions and would assure you of our expert advice entirely without obligation.

Just tell us how we can best serve you and we look forward confidently to your esteemed patronage in the future.

Yours sincerely,

RED AND WHITE ALL-BRITISH TOURS.

Although in truth Red & White were blowing their own trumpet in this preamble to their 1937 booklet nonetheless there was in those days an anxiety to do better - if only better than their competitors - but very rarely had passengers cause for complaint. It was, in the end, all down to drivers attitudes and it was sad to read in "Coachmart", 30 September 1983, "The importance of the driver was obvious - Ted Holloway told delegates that drivers were Intasun's second most common source of complaints. Drivers should be trained more thoroughly, he suggested, with that training covering the driver's attitude and obligations to his passengers as well as simply how to handle the coach competently".

ESCORTED MOTOR COACH TOURS IN GREAT BRITAIN

The coaches used on these Tours are of the luxury observation type, specially designed to provide the widest vision and equipped for really comfortable touring on the longest runs. The chauffeurs are all experienced drivers and competent mechanics.
This illustration gives an indication of the type of coach used for Tours from London. The Company reserves the right to substitute without notice coaches of alternative type and capacity should unforeseen circumstances make this necessary.

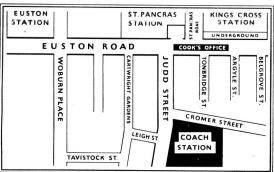

One of the fleet of " observation " coaches used for Tours from London.

Tours from LONDON start from
KING'S CROSS COACH STATION
(JUDD STREET)

USEFUL INFORMATION

Passengers are advised to be at the Motor Coach Station at least 15 minutes before departure time. Our uniformed representative will be in attendance.

What the Charge Provides.—Reserved seat in motor coach ; hotel accommodation, consisting of bedroom, breakfast and dinner at the hotels shown (or similar establishments) table d'hote luncheons and teas en route ; gratuities to hotel servants and waiters to the extent of the accommodation and meals provided ; services of a Courier throughout. Sightseeing fees are not included, but the Courier will assist in this respect for those who desire to include interior sightseeing when opportunity offers.

NOTE : If rooms with private bath are required this should be stated at time of booking, and if available they will be reserved at the appropriate supplementary charge.

Courier.—A Courier travels with each motor coach to supervise the arrangements and act as guide-lecturer, giving interesting information en route.

Baggage.—Accommodation is provided for the transport of baggage, but it will be appreciated that a reasonable limit must be enforced. Passengers should confine themselves to a single medium-size, flat suitcase each (suggested dimensions 26 ins. long, 6 ins. deep and 14 ins. wide). Steamer trunks or large bags cannot be conveyed on these tours.

Baggage Insurance.—Baggage is conveyed at owner's risk. Wise travellers will avail themselves of our Baggage Insurance, which covers risk of loss, fire, theft, or sea water damage. Insure your luggage when you book your holiday ; it takes only a moment and costs only a few shillings.

What to take with you.—Evening dress is not necessary. As there may be opportunities for sea bathing on certain tours, passengers are reminded that they may wish to pack a bathing suit. Such useful items as cameras, sun glasses, etc., should not be overlooked. Ration books are not necessary but passengers are advised to take their own soap and towels as the supplies at some hotels are still limited. Identity cards should be carried. Letters to hotels en route should be addressed c/o " Cook's Motor Tour."

SEATING PLAN OF THE COACHES NORMALLY USED ON THESE TOURS

These sketches are to show the position of the seats, and are not intended to be scale drawings.

Seating Plan for Tours 7 and 8.

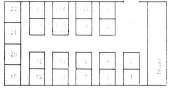

Seating Plan for Tours 1, 1A, 2, 3, 5, 5A and 6.

The aspects of touring were manifold. Each local tourist brochure advertised the facilities available for the visitor, but just as much coach company brochures and magazines carried advertisements designed with one eye on the operators requirements.

The Blue Horse Hotel appeared in a Lincs Road Car handbook - fridges are the norm now but quite rare in 1935! Simpsons Cafe had an illustrious reputation for price, translate: 3 course lunch 10p! But that is meaningless - nearer £1.50 would be right. Fish tea would, of course, incorporate locally caught fish. Court Coaches of Torquay advertised in a Midland Red Gazetteer of 1952 but dated back to charabanc days.

The 1930s "Valentine" postcard gave a fair advertisement to the coach operator, but every driver knew where the Old Forge was!

This rather battered bus of Western Welsh was, perhaps, an example of optimistic and advertising as the blind or the dented wings would neither convince customers that the company had the newest vehicles around!

In-built advertising for Northern Ireland. Seen in the lovely Mourne Mountains area of County Down on a special tour in 1953 are a pair of former U.T.A. Leyland Royal Tigers - the leading vehicle E.8930 (MZ 7965) has C36F bodywork, whilst G.8969 (OZ 842) has B42F bodywork - the latter was new that year whilst E.8930 was built in 1951.

Chapter Three

Coaching Ways - North

Red and White Services Ltd., long one of the most prestigious of companies operated tours which, while appealing to a good cross section of the public nonetheless offered not only unusual routeings, but a leisurely time. These tours are drawn from the 1937 brochure; the Mersey Tunnel 2.13 miles long (3.43 km) was opened in 1934, nine years after its commencement. The cost was £7 million and it was still a wonder of the age.

PART TWO
INCLUSIVE HOLIDAY TOURS

TOUR No. 21.   7 DAYS.

BLACKPOOL

Sheer rapture—that is Blackpool. Health, pleasure, sports, entertainments, rest and quiet, mirth and happiness, all according to individual choice and of the highest order, are certain features of this care-free holiday land on the Sea shore. It is a modern Town called into existence out of the health-giving sea breezes which stimulate great good humour, and out of the wide reaches of clean, firm, golden beach.

Leaving LONDON daily throughout the Season.

ITINERARY.

First day.—Leave London via St. Albans, Dunstable, Towcester, Daventry, Coventry, Birmingham, Walsall, Stafford, Knutsford, Preston to Blackpool.

Second Day.—Free for individual activity.

Third Day.—Whole day Tour by Motor-coach—packed lunch provided—to the famous English Lakes, embracing Keswick, Windermere, Grasmere and Derwentwater, the most beautiful scenery in England.

Fourth Day.—Free for individual activity.

Fifth Day.—Whole day Tour—packed Lunch provided—by Motor Coach to Liverpool and New Brighton, via the famous Mersey Tunnel.

Sixth Day.—Free for individual activity. Admission to the Tower or Winter Gardens provided.

Seventh Day.—After breakfast leave by coach for London via the same route as the outward journey.

Inclusive fare from London £4 19s. 6d.

The Fare includes travel by luxurious Motor-coach, accommodation at a first-class private hotel situated on the sea front with full board. Motor coach tours as above together with admission to the Winter Gardens, Pier, etc. Free Baggage Insurance, see page 8.

TOUR No. 22.   7 DAYS.

CLIFTONVILLE

TOUR No. 22 (*continued*).   7 DAYS.

With its beautiful grass-bordered paths with glorious vistas of sands and cliffs, in pleasing contrast to the formal promenades and the disturbing streams of traffic so characteristic of many seaside resorts. One can walk for miles on springy turf, almost in places reminiscent of the Downs but much more accessible and in closer proximity to the sea.

Leaving LONDON daily throughout the Season.

ITINERARY.

First Day.—Leave London via Canterbury, Sarre, Birchington, Margate to Cliftonville.

Second Day to Sixth Day.—In Cliftonville with full accommodation and the following Motor-coach Tours :—
Whole day tour to Folkestone.
Afternoon tour to St. Margaret's Bay.
Afternoon tour to Wickhambreaux.

Seventh Day.—Leave Cliftonville after lunch, by Motor-coach for London, by same route as that followed on the outward journey.

Inclusive fare from London £5 5s. 0d.

The Fare provides :—Return Motor-coach ticket London to Cliftonville, Hotel accommodation with Breakfast, Luncheon and Dinner each day, together with local tours as shown in the itinerary. Free Baggage Insurance, see page 8.

INTERIOR OF MERSEY TUNNEL, UNDER THE RIVER MERSEY, LIVERPOOL & BIRKENHEAD.

Around a couple of hundred years ago Northumberland miners wanted a tough, weatherproof, working terrier and somehow they ended up with the Bedlington. Our honeymoon couple decided they wanted to see the land of their dogs' forbears.

For many years the local operator was Bedlington & District Luxury Coaches Ltd., of Ashington, who specialised in purchasing and running other companies often elderly cast-offs. Their operations changed during the postwar period, so from the 10 double-deck buses and 7 coaches of 1957, they ended up with 21 double and 2 single deck buses in 1986, leaving their company name as somewhat of a misnomer.

Until 1930 there were seven major carriers operating on the Great North Road among them United, National, Orange Bros., Glenton Friars and Blue Band. United Automobile Services were both rapacious and quite ruthless in their (successful) attempt to gain a monopoly. The first to fall was Blue Band with Majestic, Glenton Friars, National and the guts of County Motor Services falling in 1932. Orange Brothers of Bedlington survived until July 1933, Phillipsons 1934 and Charlton 1935 were the last in that round. Timings eased, fares rose.

BEDLINGTON TERRIER

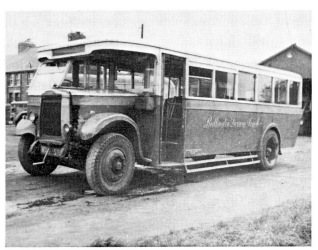

During their fight for independence Glenton Friars bought a pair of these magnificent coaches and put them on the Newcastle-London run in 1930. Bodywork was by the Hoyal Body Corporation on Daimler chassis. National Coachways (a joint venture by Glenton Friars and the directors of the Central London Coach Station) bought a further batch in 1931 but all these vehicles had gone by the end of 1934.

Passengers wanting to go by coach to Nottingham from London could have done worse than travel in an observation car of Gladwyn Parlour Car Services Ltd of Mansfield. These Dorman engined W & G vehicles were hopelessly uneconomic and this timetable of 1 September 1928 was to be the last issued, poor winter loadings leading to their liquidation - one of many to succumb in the next 7 years. Once in Nottingham, however, there was no doubt whose services one should join. From early days until quite recently Bartons were *the* name in Nottingham not least as they catered for the great population exodus from the cigarette factories and the mills during the works summer closure with literally droves of vehicles heading for Skegness and similar resorts. Although the great days are gone, only a few years ago a number of 'girls' - well into their sixties - still, out of habit, went to Sutton-on-Sea for their holidays, travelling by Barton's bus. When they ceased to travel, guest houses and hotels at Sutton became nursing homes.

Until the middle of the 1930s competition on the Manchester/London run was ruthless, being served by half-a-dozen companies: Eniway, Majestic and Roscoe among them. The route used by Majestic was typical; a meal break at 2.36 a.m. was rather sadistic.

REVISED 1st APRIL, 1933　　　　　　　**This edition cancels issue dated Dec. 1932**

MAJESTIC EXPRESS

LONDON to MANCHESTER, READ DOWN.				LONDON—MANCHESTER ROUTE and PICKING-UP POINTS	MANCHESTER to LONDON, READ UP.			
FARES from LONDON.		DAY SERVICE	NIGHT SERVICE		DAY SERVICE	NIGHT SERVICE	FARES from MANCHESTER.	
Single	Ret.						Single	Ret.
		DEPART ★		LONDON :—	ARRIVE			
		a.m.	p.m.		p.m.	a.m.		
		8.30	10.30	dep. LONDON TERMINAL COACH STATION (80, Clapham Road, nr. Oval Undgd. Station) ... arr.	★ 7.50	S 7.45		
		9.00	11.00	KING'S CROSS COACH STATION (Euston Road, King's Cross) ...	7.30	7.30	}15/-	25/-
		9.25	—	SHEPHERDS BUSH—THE LAWN...	7.10	—		
		—	11.20	FINCHLEY—" Tally. Ho " (Old Ballard's Lane) ...	—	7.11		
		10.00	—	UXBRIDGE (Canal Bridge)	6.15	—	14/6	24/-
		10.10	—	GERRARDS CROSS (The French Horn)	6.00	—	14/6	24/-
		10.20	—	BEACONSFIELD (Saracen's Head Htl.)	5.50	—	13/6	23/-
		10.35	—	HIGH WYCOMBE (Falcon Hotel) ...	5.40	—	12/6	21/-
		11.05ᴿ	—	arr. POSTCOMBE (New Inn) ... ... dep.	5.30ᵀ	—	—	—
		11.10	—	dep. ,, ,, ... arr.	5.15	—	—	—
5/-	8/6	11.45	—	OXFORD (Gloucester Green Coach Stn.)	4.35	—	11/-	19/-
7/-	12/-	12.40 L	—	arr. BANBURY (Strank's Restaurant) ...	3.40	—	10/-	17/-
		1.10	—	dep. ,, ,, ,, ...	3.40	—	10/-	17/-
9/-	14/6	1.55	—	WARWICK (Castle Hill Restaurant)	2.50	—	9/6	16/-
9/6	15/-	2.05	—	KENILWORTH (70 Warwick Road)	2.35	—	8/6	15/-
10/-	16/-	—	—	BERKSWELL (George Hotel) ... dep.	2.20	—	8/6	15/-
		—	—	,, ,, ,, arr.	1.50 L	—		
		—	11.50	ST. ALBANS (41, London Rd.) ...	—	6.41	14/-	24/-
		—	12.20	DUNSTABLE (Central Tea Rooms)...	—	6.11	13/-	23/-
4/6	7/6	—	12.48	FENNY STRATFORD (Bridge Inn)	—	5.43	12/6	21/6
5/-	8/-	—	1.06	STONY STRATFORD (High Street)	—	5.25	12/-	20/-
5/6	9/-	—	1.26	TOWCESTER (P.O. or Market Hall)...	—	5.05	11/-	18/-
7/-	11/6	—	1.56	DAVENTRY (Cross Roads, A.A. Box)	—	4.35	10/-	16/-
		—	2.36ᴿ	arr. WILLENHALL (Chace Hotel) ... dep.	—	3.57ᴿ	—	—
		—	2.56	dep. ,, ,, ... arr.	—	3.40ᴿ	—	—
9/6	15/-	—	3.00	COVENTRY (Pool Meadow)	—	3.33	9/-	15/-
10/6	16/6	3.00	3.40	arr. BIRMINGHAM — SMITHFIELD dep.	1.26	2.53		
		3.05	3.40	dep. MOTOR COACH STATION (Digbeth, arr. Near Bull Ring)	1.25	2.53	7/6	13/6
11/-	18/-	3.43	4.15	WOLVERHAMPTON (6, Market Street)	12.47	2.18	6/6	11/6
12/-	21/-	4.23	4.52	STAFFORD (Direct Coal Supply, Bridge Street, opp. Picture House)	12.07	1.41	5/6	9/3
		4.43ᵀ	5.10ᴿ	arr. DARLASTON (Darlaston Inn) ... dep.	11.47ᴿ	1.23ᴿ	—	—
		4.58ᵀ	5.23ᴿ	dep. ,, ,, ... arr.	11.42ᴿ	1.08ᴿ	—	—
13/-	22/6	5.18	5.45	NEWCASTLE. UNDER. LYME (Morgan's, Market Place)	11.22	12.48	3/6	5/6
		5.52	6.15	HOLMES CHAPEL (Red Lion Hotel)	10.48	12.18		
		6.17	6.40	KNUTSFORD (Canute Place) ...	10.23	11.53		
		6.35	6.58	ALTRINCHAM (10, The Downs) ...	10.05	11.35		
		6.40	7.03	BROADHEATH (103, Manchester Rd.)	10.00	11.30		
15/-	25/- {	6.47	7.10	SALE (89, School Road)	9.53	11.23		
		6.52	7.15	STRETFORD (1129, Chester Road) ...	9.48	11.18		
		6.57	7.20	CHORLTON (470, Wilbraham Road)	9.43	11.13		
		—	—	MANCHESTER (23, Lower Mosley St.)	9.35	11.05		
		7.10	7.30	arr. ,, (Co's. Office, 5, OXFORD RD.) dep.	9.30	11.00		
		p.m.	a.m.		a.m.	p.m.		
		★			★	S		
		READ	DOWN	L LUNCH STOP T TEA STOP R REFRESHMENT STOP	READ	UP		

★ **Sunday Day Service Coach leaves half hour later throughout**
S Saturday Night Service Coach leaves MANCHESTER half hour later. Intermediate times half hour later

A linear descendant of both the National Daimler and Gladwyn W & G observation cars was this 1½ decker built by James Whitson & Co.Ltd., of West Drayton, 31 seats of best 'bloated pluto-crat' design on a Foden rear-engined chassis which first appeared in 1950.

Mann Egerton, when in the full flush of youth, built bodies for, inter alia, Rolls Royce and their craftsmanship showed in this body on a Leyland chassis, built under Crellin-Duplex patents. The idea was to gain a great increase in seating without exceeding the regulation length and width. Insofar as it held 52 rather than the normal 33/35 the design was successful but also expensive. The arrangement if not the manufacture was simple with the 'upstairs' passengers' feet filling in the space between the 'downstairs' heads. Slightly claustrophobic despite all that glass, they were slow to load and there was inbuilt resistance among the clients to travelling with their backs to the direction of travel.

The directors of Albatross Roadways had a dream. Their dream was to carry passengers in the uttermost luxury from London to Liverpool giving them blankets, pillows, real sheets, a lavatory (between them) and a buffet service. They thought they could, somehow, find the wages of the driver and the attendant, the fuel and oil required for the Daimler sleeve valve engine and the inevitable depreciation of the Phoenix Coachworks body and contents from a payload of twelve passengers - offering bed, breakfast and transport, for only ten shillings more than the normal fare. A year later the Albatross flew no more along Britain's roads.

ALBATROSS ROADWAYS, LTD.

Phone :
City 8028/9

Reg. Office :
9/10 Pancras Lane,
E.C.4.

LIVERPOOL OFFICE
AND
TERMINUS
5 COMMUTATION ROW,
Near Lime Street Station and St. George's Hall.
opposite Wellington Monument.
Telephone North 115

A REGULAR SERVICE
— of —
SLEEPING CARS
between
LIVERPOOL & LONDON
BY ROAD,
First Class Accommodation at Third Class Fare,

THE NORTH END MOTOR TOURING CO.
(Proprietors—Mac Shane's Motors Ltd.)
5 Commutation Row, Liverpool.

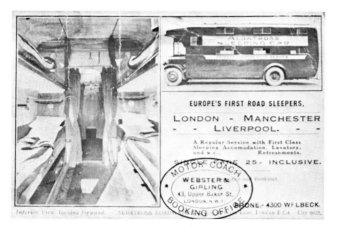

EUROPE'S FIRST ROAD SLEEPERS.
LONDON - MANCHESTER
- LIVERPOOL. -
A Regular Service with First Class
Sleeping Accomodation, Lavatory,
and w.c. Refreshments.
25/- INCLUSIVE.
WEBSTER &
GIRLING,
43, Upper Baker St.,
LONDON, N.W.1.
PHONE: 4300 WELBECK.

Whichever way one approaches Blackpool it had always seemed slightly squalid, the countryside being very far from exciting. But the arrival - ah! - that was different. Even placid coach drivers seemed almost rejuvenated by the frenetic excitement of the town.

Fred Snaylam was very proud of his coaches boasting, as he did, of their "Radio and Toilet", and although this leaflet referred to what is commonly called the Wakes Week he obviously had his eye on mill-owners' traffic rather than mill-girls, fares being pitched a few pence higher than many of his rivals. Nothing will ever recapture the atmosphere of this fantastic outward movement of the Lancashire populace during the Wakes Weeks, when even shops closed. In our case coaches were resurrected that normally mouldered in fields, cleaned up and, driven by part-timers who in winter worked as coal lorry drivers, were hired out as 'cheapies' to Blackpool.

Curiously, no photograph of any of Fred Snay-lams coaches has been traced, neither are there any illustrations available of the old "temporary" Bolton Bus Station. Fred started his operations on 24th October 1919 with a Leyland chassis registered BN 3246 and fitted with a "Char-a-banc Convertible Body, Red" and seems to have achieved a fleet maximum of six. Some of the documents relating to his coach-operating life in the 1930s have survived and shed some light on attitudes of the time.

19th May, 1932

In the Notices and Proceedings of the Traffic Commissioners for the North Western Area dated the 14th instant the following decision appears:-

To. F. Snaylam, Bolton, to operate a service of express carriages between Farnworth and Blackpool. Granted Solely in the character of excursions and tours. To be operated at inclusive return fares. No single tickets to be booked. Newport Street, Bolton, to be deleted as a picking up point. Moor Lane 'Bus Station, Bolton, to be the only point used.

The license as you will observe from the above is really in the character of one for excursions and tours though it has been granted as an express carriage license to enable the operator to book passengers for period returns, some doubt as to whether such bookings could properly be made under an excursions and tours license having been expressed by the chairman of the Traffic Commissioners.

31st March, 1932

Markets Superintendent,
Market Hall,
Bolton.

Dear Sir,

I should be pleased if you will give me permission to use the platform on the Moor Lane Bus Station for the picking up of passengers, in connection with my Express Service to Blackpool, Lytham and St. Annes, twice daily at 10. a.m. and 2 p.m.

Hoping you will consider my application at your earliest convenience.

Yours faithfully,
(Signed) F. Snaylam

May 2nd, 1938

The Market Superintendent,
County Borough of Bolton,
Market Superintendent's Office,
Ashburner Street,
BOLTON.

Dear Sir,

re BOOKING OFFICE AT MOOR LANE 'BUS STATION.

I beg to inform you that consequent upon the sale of my business to Ribble Motor Services Ltd., and the Lancashire United Transport & Power Co. Ltd., I ask that my present tenancy of the Moor Lane booking office together with the right of running vehicles from the ground immediately adjoining, be transferred to Ribble Motor Services Ltd., who wish to take it over subject to the exact terms under which I now hold it.

Trusting this meets with your approval.

Yours faithfully,

(Signed) F. SNAYLAM

JOINT SERVICE

The Liverpool road from London has always been overcrowded, but anyone who has made the overnight trip on a Standerwick ECW semi-coach will know why the railways never really suffered much competition.   Imperial chose to give its customers a country tour; in keeping would be for the customers to take tea at Ye Olde Malt Tea House.   The tram is typically Birmingham, 3'6" gauge.

Ye Olde Malt Tea House.
Built A.D. 1425

Amersham, Buckinghamshire
From a Drawing by W.P. Robins R.E.

ROUTE, TIME TABLE & FARE.	Day	Night	Single	Return
London Terminal Coaching Stn Tel Reliance 1281	9.40	10.30		
Thomas Saloon Coach, 4, Eccleston St.				
Coach Travels Ltd., Vauxhall Bridge Rd.	10.0	10.45		
Parnens ,, ,, ,,				
Embankment (morning)				
Golden Cross Hotel, Strand (night)				
BUSH HOUSE ALDWYCH	10.25	10.55		
Road Travel Booking Tem. Bar 5801.	10.30	11.0		
IMPERIAL LONDON OFFICE				
50, Southampton Row. Mus. 1808				
Rymer's Victoria House ,, ,,	10.35			
McShanes, 53. Woburn Place W.C.1.	10.50	11.10		
London Central Station, Cartwright Gds (night				
London Control O. 8, York Rd., Kings X	10.50	11.20		
Portman Travel Bureau, 27 Edgware Rd.	11.0	11.0		
West London Booking Office, 41 Goldhawk Rd.	11.10			
Sports Supply. 165 King Street Hammersmith				
Acton				
Ealing 9, New Broadway	11.30			
Hillingdon				
Hanwell 188, Uxbridge Rd.				
Southall Goodman, 15, Broadway.				
Uxbridge Coachs, 159, High St.	12.0			
Gerrards Cross				
BEACONSFIELD	12.10			
High Wycombe	12.30		2/6	5/-
West Wycombe				
STOKENCHURCH				
Postcombe	1.10			
Tetsworth				
OXFORD Music Stores, High Street.	1.35		4/6	8/6
Woodstock	1.48			
Enstone				
Chipping Norton			6/6	12/-
Long Compton				
Shipston on Stour				
Tredington				
Newbold on Stour				
STRATFORD-on-**AVON** Blue Bus Company	2.40		9/-	17/-
WARWICK	3.10		,,	,,
KENILWORTH	3.14		,,	,,
George in the Tree				
Stonebridge	3.30		,,	,,
BIRMINGHAM "Erdington" Tram Terminus.	3.40		9/-	17/-
Sutton Coldfield.				
Coleshill				
LICHFIELD Franter, 17, St. Johns St.	3.45		11/-	20/-
Rugeley.	4.13			
Gt. Hayward	4.25			
Stone				
STAFFORD	5.0		12/-	22/-
Darlaston				
Tittensor				
Trentham				
NEWCASTLE-under-Lyme Morgon 16, Pankall St.	5.37		13/-	24/-
Talke,				
Holmes Chapel	6.10			
Knutsford Bywaters Cafe	6.27			
Stockton Heath, Endersby's Victoria Garage.				
WARRINGTON Richardson 69, Bridge St.	6.54		15/-	25/-
Prescot 1, Derby St.				
LIVERPOOL Hughes Hotel Old Haymarket.	7.20	7.30	15/-	27/6

IMPERIAL MOTOR SERVICES   Tel. 787 Royal.   308, Upper Parliament St.   *Children under Twelve two-thirds full fare.*   *Sundays at same times.*   *All times Approximate.*

A TRIP TO LIVERPOOL

includes some of the finest country to be seen in any part of the world.

We pass out of London via Acton-Ealing into the old-world towns and villages round the metropolis.

Uxbridge with its quaint market place marks the outlying boundary of London and the termination of the trams and we Pass through many well-known landmarks until we reach **Beaconsfield**, the charming rural town where the great Disraeli lived and from which he took his title.

The picturesque lanes lead to the busy town of **High Wycombe**, famed for manufacture of chairs and for its quaint streets, the Falcon Inn for its noted generous fare is our stopping place here if required.

Stokenchurch, has a pleasant view.

We arrive next at **Oxford** with its beautiful University buildings, famous alike for its learning and history. It is with regret that we have such a brief time at so interesting a spot, but we must continue our journey until we reach **Woodstock** with Blenheim Palace, the home of the Marlboroughs, its rustic cottages and beautiful undulating streets

Thirty miles bring us to Stratford-on-Avon' the birthplace of the greatest bard in all the world. If there is time, a glimpse of Shakespeare's birthplace may be obtained, but the little town is worthy of a full day's stay to view Shakepeare's house, Anne Hathaways's cottage at Shottery, the beautiful river and the surrounding wonderful country teeming with interest. A stay for a day can be arranged if so desired by giving notice at time of booking.

Warwick with its castle and gateways and many interesting features of the Middle Ages take our attention until kenilworth is reached, where the ruins form the centre of attraction, a picture not to be easily forgotten. A local guide can be obtained to give all information if you are staying in the Shakespeare country for any time. We pass along the Chester Road by Erdington, the suburb of Birmingham and Walsall with their teeming populations both claim interest until the old world town of **Lichfield** with its mediæval and interesting Cathedral attracts attention; next you pass through the potteries to the open country and arrive at the undulating country of Cheshire which merges into the industrial area of Lancashire and brings you to **Warrington** and finally to **Liverpool** with its many attractions—eg. Docks, Museums with a with a magnificent collection of pictures, St. Georges Hall, built in the Grecian style Cathedral, etc., completes a journey of interest, information and experience.

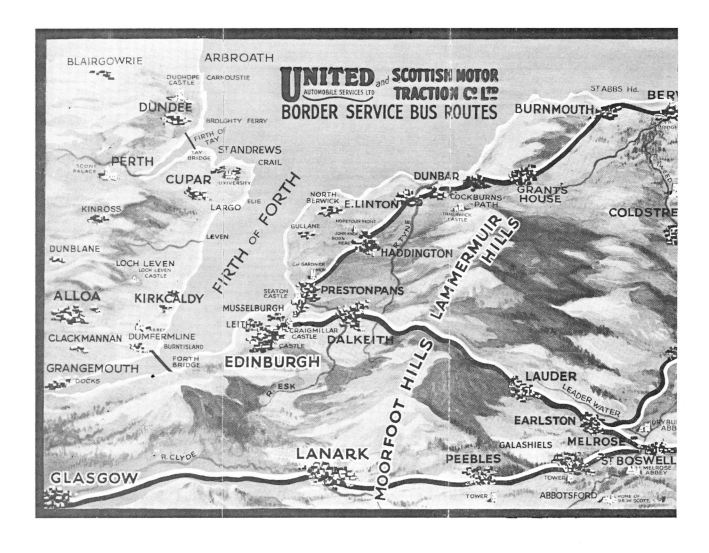

Western SMT were one of the 'reliable' concerns in Scotland, and their post-war timetable shows a mixture of meticulous and vague timings. Did they really expect, quite often elderly, passengers to make use of the facilities at Lymes Cafe, Grantham (bearing in mind the inevitable queues at the 'Ladies') and eat some sort of meal (which one may guess would be far too hot and the service sluggish) in a mere 20 minutes when the brain is dazed at 12.26 a.m.? But one arrives at precisely 10.54 outward and 11.54 inward - or at least "abt" this time! The coach represents the fleet, neat, quite plain but comfortable.

This leaflet is in colour and an unusual approach to the subject.

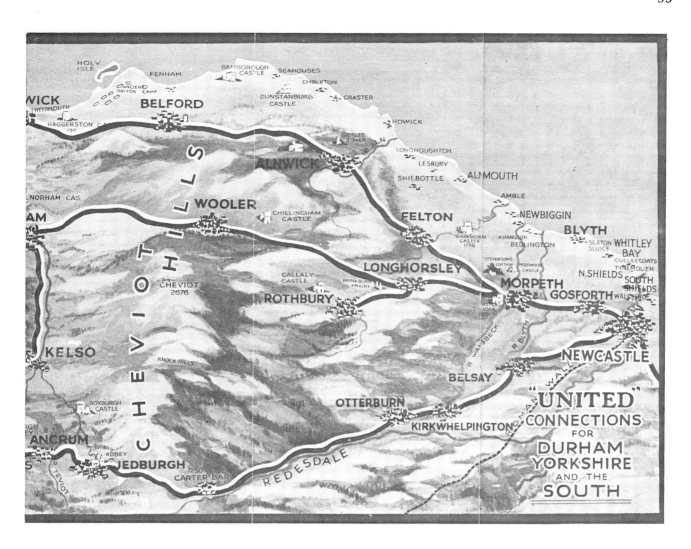

GLASGOW		LONDON
Southward Journey	– TIME TABLE –	Northward Journey

		p.m.			p.m.
Glasgow (Buchanan St. Bus Station)... depart		7 00	London (Victoria Coach Station) . depart		8 00
Hamilton (Excelsior Agency, New Cross) ..		7 30	Baldock (Alnott's Cafe)		9 41
Gretna (Union Jack Hotel) ... ... ,,		10 18	Stamford (Square)		11 43
Carlisle (Blair & Palmers' Garage) ... ,,		10 35			a.m.
Carlisle (Bus Station, Lowther Street and			Grantham (Post Office)		12 21
Country Cafe) ... ... arrive		10 38	Grantham (Lymes Cafe)... ... ... arrive		12 26
Carlisle (Bus Station, Lowther Street) ... depart		10 58	Grantham (Lymes Cafe)... ... . depart		12 46
Penrith (Crown Hotel)		11 43	Doncaster (Fisher's Cafe) ... ... ,,		2 41
		a.m.	Boroughbridge (Kelly's Cafe) ... ... ,,		3 21
Boroughbridge (Kelly's Cafe) ... ... ,,		2 33	Penrith (Crown Hotel)		7 11
Doncaster (Fisher's Cafe) ... ... ,,		4 13	Carlisle (Bus Station, Lowther Street and		
Grantham (Lymes Cafe)... ... ... arrive		6 08	Country Cafe) ... ... arrive		7 56
Grantham (Lymes Cafe)... ... ... depart		6 28	Carlisle (Bus Station, Lowther Street) ... depart		8 16
Grantham (Post Office) ... ... ,,		6 32	Carlisle (Blair & Palmers' Garage)		8 19
Stamford (Square)		7 11	Gretna (Union Jack Hotel) ... ... ,,		8 36
Baldock (Alnott's Cafe) ... ... ,,		9 13	Hamilton (Excelsior Agency, New Cross) depart		11 24
London (Victoria Coach Station) ...arr. abt.		10 54	Glasgow (Buchanan St. Bus Station).. arr. abt.		11 54

FARES (Principal Fares) LIST

	Single	Return		Single	Return
Glasgow – Boroughbridge 18/-			London – Carlisle 27/-		45/-
Glasgow—Doncaster 21/-		40/-	London—Penrith 26/-		43/-
Glasgow—Grantham 26/-		43/-	London—Lockerbie 30/-		50/-
Glasgow—London 30/-		50/-			

CHILDREN over 3 and under 14 years of age—Half of Adult Fare to nearest threepence.

CONDITIONS

BOOKINGS:—Passengers on Booking Return Tickets must apply at the same time for seat reservation for the Return Journey.

LUGGAGE:—Passengers allowed 40 lbs. personal luggage free, limited in size to 26 in. x 18 in. x 12 in. The Company do not hold themselves responsible for loss or damage to any kind of luggage. Passengers are recommended to insure luggage.

36

EXCURSIONS BY STAGE CARRIAGE SERVICES

Daily except Sundays

FORT WILLIAM

	a.m.	a.m.		p.m.	p.m.
Inverness........dep.	8.15	11.15	Fort William ...dep.	2.50	5.30
Fort William ... arr.	11.0	2.50p	Inverness ....arr.	5.35	8.20

DAY RETURN FARE 13/-

FORT AUGUSTUS

Leave at 8.15 a.m., 11.15 a.m. and 3.30 p.m. | Returning from Fort Augustus at 1.30 p.m., 4.10 p.m., 6.55 p.m.

FARE 8/-

DRUMNADROCHIT

Leave at 8.15 a.m., 10.30 a.m. (Sats. only), 11.15 a.m., 1.0 p.m., 4.0 p.m. | Returning from Drumnadrochit at 11.43 a.m., 12.55 p.m. (Sats. only), 1.55 p.m., 2.57 p.m., 4.57 p.m., 5.20 p.m. (Sats. only), 7.42 p.m.

FARE 3/7

FOYERS

Leave at 11.0 a.m., 1.0 p.m. (Weds. only), 2.40 p.m. (Sats. only), 4.15 p.m. (except Sats.). | Returning from Foyers at 1.15 p.m., 4.30 p.m. (Sats. only), 5.45 p.m. (except Sats.), 7.20 p.m. (Sats. only).

FARE 4/2

ALL COACHES DEPART FROM FARRALINE PARK (off Academy Street)

TOURS THROUGH
THE WESTERN HIGHLANDS AND ISLANDS

(Ask for illustrated brochure giving full particulars.)

All Passengers and their luggage are conveyed subject to the Company's Conditions of Shipment as specified in Sailing Bills.

DAVID MACBRAYNE, LIMITED
33 QUEENSGATE INVERNESS

Head Office:—CLYDE HOUSE, 44 Robertson Street, GLASGOW, C.2

JOHN HORN, LTD., GLASGOW

David MacBrayne had a well deserved reputation and despite their almost total monopoly, always offered a good class of tour. The rather set-piece (if not naive) drawing from an SMT leaflet of the late 1930s showed the type of middle class clientele they set out to attract. Incidentally, MacBraynes fares were not low, the Oban tour in today's money costing at least £10, the Three Glens £6.25 or so.

WHAT TOUR SHALL WE TAKE THIS SUMMER?

Not all is as it seems. Although the excursion leaflet is entirely genuine in September 1928, the photograph is not. The Devil's Elbow, Glen Shee, certainly looked like this in the early 1950s but the coach has almost without doubt been super-imposed, unless Mr. Tilling really wanted his name as a mirror image. Whether, too, the gradient really was 1 in 3 is doubtful, although my ex-WD Matchless motorcycle needed pushing and don't the midges love innocents abroad!

NEGOTIATING THE TOP BEND OF THE DEVIL'S ELBOW, GLENSHEE. THE HIGHEST PUBLIC ROAD IN BRITAIN, ALTITUDE 2000 FEET. STEEPEST GRADIENT 1 IN 3

Among the more unusual tour operators were Northern General. The design of these vehicles was, to say the least, unusual and they represent a maverick line of thought. Sixty-eight members of classes SE6 (side-engine 6 wheeler) and SE4 (2 axle) were completed. 652 is brand new, and seated 28 within her 30'0" (9.14m) length and 10'0" (3.05m) height. By 1950 727 is showing her 14 years of wear, her six cylinder Hercules petrol engine had long been replaced by an AEC 7.7 oiler; vibration did little to improve the joints in her Beadle of Dartford body.

United publicity always had a certain charm, this leaflet being printed in red and green on a cream background. Even their little 'points' carried a promise that service would be good, although with competition gone United became just another monopolistic carrier.

"In this folder are particulars of departure times and fares in respect of the luxury coach services of United, Majestic, Orange and Phillipsons to London. In addition to the three primary points of comfort, convenience and economy which have made for the popularity of these services, there is one other inherent factor which should be called to mind - ROAD TRAVEL IS INTIMATE TRAVEL. It takes you through the heart of the land; you never lose touch with the interest and loveliness it contains. The days of uncomfortable road travel have gone for ever - now the passenger sits back at ease, and views a changing scene of never-failing charm . . . The cafes at which coaches stop have been inspected, and appetising food at reasonable prices may be obtained at the places mentioned in the timetable. Menus will be passed around the coaches before arrival at each refreshment stop to enable passengers to make an early choice. Heaters are fitted, and cushions may be hired for 6d, [2½p] each per journey".

However a couple of years later, "The issue of a ticket to a passenger does not guarantee any particular seat in a Coach, or a seat in any particular Coach. Seats should be booked not less than 48 hours before departure". The recent railway difficulties with space availability gives one a feeling of deja vu!

The coach is an AEC Regal, the body by Harringtons.

Many times a question asked is why Mrs. Hilda Thatcher (Conservative Prime Minister) has always favoured road traffic over rail or canal. One answer could be that as a child she rode on this all Leyland TS7 Tiger of Western SMT. Seen here in 1935, the vehicle, one of 29 built, is about to depart from Grantham to Glasgow. This coach represented the unashamed luxury both inside and out that road operators necessarily offered to compete with railway speed. This coupled with low fares would have been just the ticket for Mrs. T's family!

The arrival of our coach into Newcastle was almost invariably by means of the Tyne Bridge. The four white topped vehicles are presumably local service buses but the coach has both luggage on its roofrack and, to show the slow speeds then in force, a bicyclist has hung on the back for a lift.

Leyland TS7 Tiger of Western SMT

The Hunting Country

The south-west corner of Lincolnshire and those portions of the neighbouring counties of Leicestershire, Nottinghamshire and Rutlandshire which lie between Grantham and Leicester and Nottingham and Stamford, have long been famous as the premier " hunting country " in the land. A rolling, undulating, well wooded country, free from industrial centres and a truly rural area. It is a district rich in fine estates and stately country houses, and offers many attractive views to charm the eye of the wayfarer. Right in the centre of this area is MELTON MOWBRAY, famous not only as a hunting centre, but also for its Stilton cheese and pork pies. Of the great estates BELVOIR CASTLE, lying between Grantham and Melton Mowbray, is the most magnificent of them all. This is the country seat of the Duke of Rutland. The present building is comparatively modern, having been erected after the destruction of the previous castle by fire in 1816. At certain times the beautiful gardens and portions of the wonderful building are open for inspection.

Over the Lincolnshire border lies GRANTHAM, an ancient town which has been greatly modernized and developed industrially. No visitor to the town should miss the great and beautiful Church of St. Wulfram, a grand and beautiful building. It was commenced about 1250 and completed about two centuries later. Another town just inside the Lincolnshire border is the quaint old-world town of STAMFORD. This is one of the best preserved of our ancient towns, though it has been the scene of many stirring conflicts at various periods of its history. The town is remarkable for its wealth of churches and ancient buildings, and only a few minutes' walk from the centre of the town is Burghley House and Park—the seat of the Marquis of Exeter. The magnificent park, with its wonderful avenues of fine trees, and the stately mansion are open to visitors on certain days of the week.

Paddy's Market, Quayside, Newcastle c.1925 situated under Tyne Bridge. This was one of the famous tourist attractions of Newcastle and one our honeymoon couple would long have remembered. Overhead on Stephenson's Bridge a steam engine runs light to the station.

Chapter Four

Capital Coaching

In 1956 Black & White Coaches (Walthamstow) together with their subsidiary Majestic Luxury Coaches were absorbed by George Ewer & Co - Grey-Green Coaches. In happier days a so new it is not even registered Duple bodied Leyland was photographed outside the coach-builders' works.

By way of contrast (below) the Seagull body on the St. Helens Industrial Cooperative Society's coach compares with the luxurious Harrington Wayfarer I fitted to Orange Luxury Coaches machine.

Coincidentally, Orange too, were absorbed by Grey Green.

Obviously competiton on the coast roads out of London was fantastic with not only the road vehicles competing with one another but the constituent parts of the Southern Railway also engaged in internicine war. The punter (those who didn't spend the day by the roadside, for vehicle breakdowns were commonplace) gained to an almost unbelievable extent. In 1926 the Holiday Coaches Company using Studebaker 14 and 18 seaters charged 14/- (70p) for a day trip to Hastings, by April 1928 South London Coaches operating 26-seater Lancias had brought it down to 8/- (40p) and in 1936 Valliant Direct, with AEC Regals charged 6/6d (32½p); prices that must have given marginal profits at best.

The Better Way—Travel

VALLIANT
DIRECT
TO THE COAST

AUTUMN FARES

In operation on and after Sept. 14th (to Sept. 30th) *1936*

COAST RESORT	REDUCED FARES			FROM THE COAST	
	Single	Day Ret.	Period Ret.	Point	Time
BRIGHTON	4/6	5/-	8/6	Hippodrome Garage Middle Street.	6.00 p.m.
WORTHING	5/6	6/6	9/6	Norfolk Hotel	5.45 p.m.
LITTLEHAMPTON	6/-	7/-	10/6	The Library Maltravers Road.	5.20 p.m.
BOGNOR	6/-	7/-	10/6	Motor Coach Park Gloucester Road.	5.00 p.m.
CANTERBURY	4/6	6/-	8/6	Level Crossing	5.30 p.m.
MARGATE	5/6	6/6	10/-	Motor Coach Park All Saints Road.	4.40 p.m.
RAMSGATE	5/6	6/6	10/-	Foxs Garage King Street.	4.30 p.m.
EASTBOURNE	5/6	6/6	9/6	Motor Coach Park Susan's Road.	5.30 p.m.
BEXHILL	5/6	6/6	10/-	Town Hall Square	5.10 p.m.
HASTINGS	5/6	6/6	10/-	Motor Coach Park Fish Market.	5.00 p.m.
PORTSMOUTH	6/-	7/6	10/6	St. Michael's Road (Victroia Hall).	5.35 p.m.
SOUTHSEA	6/-	7/6	10/6	Motor Coach Park Clarence Pier.	5.30 p.m.
SOUTHAMPTON	5/6	7/-	10/-	Grosvenor Square	5.45 p.m.
BOURNEMOUTH	9/-	10/6	15/-	Motor Coach Station 77 Holdenhurst Rd.	4.30 p.m.
*YARMOUTH	8/-	12/6	14/-	Cantab Coach Stat'n 5 Marine P'de Cent	4.15 p.m.
*LOWESTOFT	8/-	12/6	14/-	The Car Park Battery Green.	4.00 p.m.

* Operating Fridays, Saturdays, Sundays and Mondays only.

CHILDREN HALF FARE

Departure Times from **Your** District to the Coast are shown overleaf.

Book at 38 Uxbridge Road, W. 5.

or at your Local Agent :

**GOUGH'S TRAVEL
1 NORTH AUDLEY ST.
GROSVENOR SQ. W.1.**

NOTE. This Leaflet is issued as a supplement to the SUMMER HANDBILL and the Regulations respecting Conditions of Tickets and Travel by this Company are as detailed on the Summer Handbills.

SOUTH LONDON COACHES

Head Office : 137 ELEPHANT ROAD, S.E.17
'Phone : RODNEY 3805-6

EASTER AND SPRING PROGRAMME

MOTOR COACH SERVICES AND AFTERNOON TOURS

Commencing FRIDAY, APRIL 6th, 1928

LOCAL AGENT

When booking please ask to travel by
SOUTH LONDON COACHES
ALL SEATS NUMBERED AND RESERVED

44

Day tours around London were always obligatory for American visitors, such excursions being operated by a myriad of small concerns and even in the strictly regulated 1950s it was not uncommon for door-keepers of the not-quite-top-notch hotels to be propositioned with the use of a 20-seater so-called 'taxi' for his clients. And what was there to see - oh! "the world and his ways!"

TOUR No. 44.   AFTERNOON.

West End Sight-seeing Tour

Leaving Royal Hotel, Woburn Place at 2.30 p.m. daily throughout the Year.

We pass through the smartest shopping centre of London, via Piccadilly Circus, Regent Street, Oxford Street (large departmental stores), Hyde Park, the Smallest House in London, the Pet's Cemetery, Kensington, the Albert Hall, the Albert Memorial, the Albert Museum, Brompton Oratory, Harrods ; on to Chelsea and then the Abbey, where we visit the Royal Chapels (containing the tombs of the most important Kings of England), the Cloisters, the Poet's Corner, and the Unknown Warrior's Grave, Trafalgar Square, etc.

Inclusive Fare, 6/6.   20 miles Trip with Guide Lecturer.

TOUR No. 45.   EVENING.

Chinatown and the East End

Leaving Royal Hotel, Woburn Place at 8 p.m. daily throughout the Year.

Passing Staple Inn, Smithfield Market, St. Bartholomew's Hospital, Charles Dickens' House, St. Giles, Cripple Gate (Milton), Roman Wall, Wesley's Chapel at Bunhill (Bone Hill), Shoreditch, Whitechapel, the Ghetto, People's Palace, Charlie Brown's, Rotherhithe Tunnel, Southwark, places frequented by Charles Dickens, the " Old George " Inn, etc. Soho.

Inclusive Fare, 6/-.   20 miles Trip with Guide Lecturer.

3.   LONDON LIFE : The Busy Docks in the Port of London.

LUDGATE CIRCUS, LONDON, E.C.4

TOUR No. 46.   AFTERNOON.

Windsor & Eton Colleges

Leaving Royal Hotel, Woburn Place at 2.15 p.m. every after-noon throughout the Season.

Hyde Park, Notting Hill, Chiswick, the Great West Road, Coln-brook (" Ye Ostrich Feathers " Inn), Windsor Castle, visit the Grounds and the magnificent St. George's Chapel (State apartments optional), Eton College—1440—(visit of the class rooms optional), Runnymede —1215—Slough, Staines, the wonderful Hampton Court Gardens, Bushey Park. Time permitting we also visit Stoke Poges, the home of the Penn Family.

Inclusive fare, 10/-.   80-mile Round Trip with Guide Lecturer.

The number of passengers we took on tours of Windsor Castle and Eton boggles the mind with every tongue on the earth wishing to see 'Her Majesty' (some colonials distinctly lésé, others of Middle Eastern origin clearly wishing they had a smoking bomb with them).   The RFW class of coaches built for LT with bodywork by Eastern Coach Works on Regal IV chassis were rather uninspired in design (and probably based on Thomas Tilling equivalents) functional, and com-fortable enough for short tours.   The RF class of which there were 700 had even less luxury, serving (in various paint and trim finishes) as Central London and Country Buses, Green Line coaches and - despite bus seats - tour coaches.   The best way to see London though was from a trolley bus, high, quiet and surprisingly varied in its routes and clientele.

The Birch family first appeared in the London Road transport business in 1832, operating cabs from Westminster. Then followed horse buses; after various vicissitudes the company of Birch Brothers Ltd., was founded in 1899, motor bus work commencing in 1904. This Bedford service commenced in November 1928 and was consolidated in 1932 when Beaumont Safeway coaches were bought out.

All Birch's internal London workings were lost on 21 February 1934 when the London Passenger Transport Board used their powers of compulsory acquisition. Incidentally, the LPTB were basically busmen, eliminating trams as soon as they could. Birch Brothers thrived until 1968 when their country services were sold off, the 'main line' to Rushden following in 1969. February 1971 saw the end of the line when the remaining assets were sold to George Ewer (the Grey-Green Group).

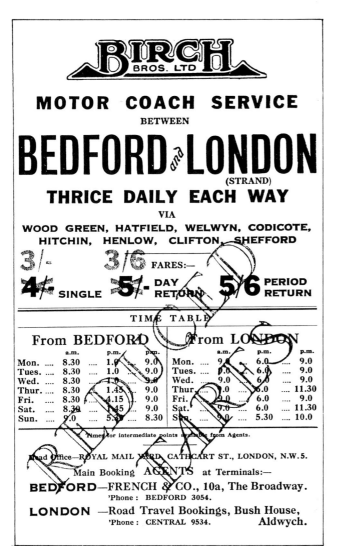

Cancelling all previous issues.   **Subject to alteration without notice.**

BEAUMONT-SAFEWAY

TRAVEL   ## SALOON COACHES.   **TRAVEL**

BY

Commencing 28th, March 1931
Improved Services Between
Leighton Buzzard, Dunstable
BY

ROAD   AND ## LONDON OXFORD CIRCUS & KINGS CROSS   **ROAD**

via HOCKLIFFE, DUNSTABLE, MARKYATE, REDBOURN AND ST. ALBANS.

WEEKDAYS

Leave LEIGHTON BUZZARD.		Leave DUNSTABLE		Leave LONDON			
				OXFORD	CIRCUS	KINGS	CROSS
North St. Garage	7.45 a.m.	Central Tea Rooms	8.15 a.m.	281, Regent St.	10.15 a.m.	Railway Street	10.30 a.m.
,, ,,	9.0 a.m	,, ,,	9.30 a.m.	To Dunstable only	† 1.45 p.m.	To Dunstable only	† 2.0 p.m.
,, ,,	1.30 p.m.	,, ,, (Mon to Frid only)	2.0 p.m.	,, ,,	3.45 p.m,	,, ,,	4.0 p.m.
,, ,, (Saturdays only)	4.0 p.m.	(Saturdays only)	4.0 p.m.				
North St. Garage		(Saturdays only)	4.30 p m.	281, Regent St.	5.45 p.m.	Railway Street	6.0 a.m.
,, ,,	8.0 p.m.	Central Tea Rooms	6.0 p.m.	,, ,,	* 7.45 p m.	,, ,,	* 8.0 p.m.
,, ,,		,, ,, (Saturdays only	8.30 p.m.	,, ,,	9.45 p.m.	,, ,,	10 0 p.m.
			10.0 p.m.				

† Saturdays only to LEIGHTON BUZZARD.   * On Saturdays to DUNSTABLE Only

SUNDAYS.

Leave LEIGHTON BUZZARD.		Leave DUNSTABLE.		Leave LONDON.			
				OXFORD	CIRCUS	KINGS	CROSS
North St. Garage.	8.30 a.m.	Central Tea Rooms	9.0 a.m.	281, Regent St.	8.45 a.m.	Railway Street	9.0 a.m.
,, ,,	11.0 a.m.	,, ,,	11.30 a.m.	,, ,,	10.15 a.m.	,, ,,	10.30 a.m.
,, ,,	5.30 p.m.	,, ,,	6.0 p.m.	,, ,,	5.45 p.m.	,, ,,	6.0 p.m.
,, ,,	8.0 p.m.	,, ,,	8.30 p.m.	,, ,,	* 7.15 a.m.	,, ,,	* 7.30 p.m.
		,, ,,	9.30 p.m.	,, ,,	9.45 p m.	,, ,,	10.0 p.m.
				,, ,,	11.15 p.m.	,, ,,	11.30 p.m.

* To DUNSTABLE only

EASTER MONDAY APRIL 6th Sunday Time-table will be operated.

FARES

	Single	Day Return	Period Return
LEIGHTON BUZZARD to LONDON	3/-	4/-	5/6
DUNSTABLE to LONDON	2/-	3/-	3/6
ST ALBANS ,, ,,	1/6	2/-	3/-

MAIN AGENTS AND STOPPING POINTS

LEIGHTON BUZZARD North Street Garage   Phone : 43
HOCKLIFFE Post Office   Phone 1
DUNSTABLE Central Tea Rooms   Phone :234
MARKYATE Neal's Stores
REDBOURN H. Halsey, 78, High Street
ST, ALBANS T. Hansell, 41, London Road
BARNET Barnet Travel Bureau, 116, High St.   Phone: Barnet 0433
NORTH FINCHLEY Ideal Tea Rooms, 17, High Street   Phone : Hillside 3141
(Tally Ho Corner)
EAST FINCHLEY Weedon's Travel Bureau, 34, High Rd. Phone: Tudor 2080
HIGHGATE Highgate Booking Office, 2, Archway Rd. Phone : Archway 2251
(Archway Tavern) Weedon's Travel Bureau, 82, Junction Rd. Phone Archway 1656
LONDON Toveys 4, York Road.   Phone : North 0118
Highways' Booking Office, 281, Regent Street, W.1.

AND ALL LONDON BOOKING AGENTS.

VICTORIA BOOKING OFFICE, Vauxhall Bridge Road, S.W.

Priest Bros. Printers. 225. Philip Lane. Tottenham. N.15

An interesting 'combination' advertisement from Bus & Coach, January 1962. In this particular model an AEC Reliance is used as the chassis, but only British makes appear. Not entirely coincidentally we find AEC selling out to Leyland six months after this advertisement appeared. Willowbrook seems no longer independent having sold out to Duple four years earlier but this Viscount styling did little to help sales. The "new style cutaway rear end" shown here was similar, insofar as it had a reverse rake rear window, to that of the Ford Anglia 105E saloon; significantly both 'dated' quickly, and the designs were not picked up by other manufacturers. Incidentally in 1971 the Willowbrook name was purchased from Duple and regained its independence. But the primary beneficiary of this advertisement must surely have been Birch Brothers; free and gratis publicity!

WILLOWBROOK VISCOUNT

41 passenger luxury coach

TRAVEL IN THE FUTURE

Designed for long-distance travel at high speeds, here is a coach with a future . . a coach that adds a new conception to luxury travel ! Today's Willowbrook Viscount reflects *tomorrow's* trends in design, styling and comfort. Distinguishing features include double curvature front screens fitted with demisters and wide side windows to aid all-round visibility. Add to this superb interior finish to ensure passenger comfort plus *proven* reliability and worth in terms of efficiency, safety and economical operation. What more could any progressive operator want? You can choose between having the new style cutaway rear end or one of conventional design. Yes, the Willowbrook Viscount could well be the answer to *your* fleet extension or replacement problem. Why not get fuller particulars today? *Chassis:* A.E.C. Reliance, Leyland Tiger Cub or Leopard.

Willowbrook is a Duple Group Company . . . a member of Britain's leading coach building organization. It is the policy of the Duple Group that each of the companies within its framework continues to retain its own, individual production whilst, at the same time, offering wider service and repair facilities. This addition to efficiency is yet another advantage of operating with coaches built by the Group.

DUPLE DRIVES AHEAD ... *for years and years to come*

All Sales Enquiries to:—

 **DUPLE GROUP SALES LIMITED**

THE SALES ORGANIZATION FOR DUPLE ● BURLINGHAM ● WILLOWBROOK

Edgware Rd., The Hyde, London, N.W.9. Tel. COLindale 6412.
Repair & Service at Duple Group Factories: Duple Motor Bodies Ltd., The Hyde, London, N.W.9. Tel. COL 6412. Duple Motor Bodies (Mid.) Ltd. and Willowbrook Ltd., Swingbridge Rd., Loughborough. Tel. 4541. H. V. Burlingham Ltd., New House Rd., Blackpool. Tel. 62251

Chapter Five

Coaching Ways - South by East

The ultimate expression of B.M.M.O. inventiveness and forward looking approach came on Monday 2 November 1959 when the first motorway in Britain (the M1) was opened and Midland Red was there, with the necessary licences and brand new vehicles - the justly famous CM5T (T = toilet) class.   For just a short while badges were polished and jackets pressed as drivers basked in reflected glory.   This is the winter 1963 timetable.

THE SYMBOL OF SERVICE

MOTORWAY EXPRESS SERVICES

TIMETABLES

DAILY (Except Christmas Day)

BIRMINGHAM to LONDON

		a.m.	p.m.	p.m.
BIRMINGHAM (DIGBETH COACH STATION)	depart	8.30	2.00	6.30
LONDON (VICTORIA COACH STATION)	arrive	11.25	4.55	9.25

LONDON to BIRMINGHAM

		a.m.	p.m.	p.m.
LONDON (VICTORIA COACH STATION)	depart	9.30	1.30	6.30
BIRMINGHAM (DIGBETH COACH STATION)	arrive	12.25	4.25	9.25

FARES   17/9 Single   26/3 Day Return   30/- Period Return
(SATURDAYS—Whit Saturday to end of September inclusive)
(19/6 Single   29/- Day Return   33/3 Period Return)

DAILY (Except Christmas Day)

NUNEATON and COVENTRY to LONDON

		a.m.	p.m.	p.m
NUNEATON (BUS STATION)	depart	8.00	1.30	6.30
BEDWORTH (MARKET PLACE)	depart	8.10	1.40	6.40
COVENTRY (POOL MEADOW)	arrive	8.30	2.00	7.00
COVENTRY (POOL MEADOW)	depart	8.40	2.10	7.10
LONDON (VICTORIA COACH STATION	arrive	11.00	4.30	9.30

LONDON to COVENTRY and NUNEATON

		a.m.	p.m.	p.m.
LONDON (VICTORIA COACH STATION)	depart	9.00	12.30	7.00
COVENTRY (POOL MEADOW)	arrive	11.20	2.50	9.20
COVENTRY (POOL MEADOW)	depart	11.30	3.00	9.30
BEDWORTH (MARKET PLACE)	arrive	11.50	3.20	9.50
NUNEATON (BUS STATION)	arrive	12.00	3.30	10.00

FARES   Nuneaton—London Single : 17/3   Day Return : 25/3   Period Return : 28/6
Bedworth—London   16/9   24/3   27/3
Coventry—London   16/-   23/3   26/3

(SATURDAYS—Whit Saturday to end of September inclusive
Nuneaton—London Single : 19/-   Day Return : 27/9   Period Return : 31/-
Bedworth—London   18/6   26/9   30/-
Coventry—London   18/-   25/9   29/-)

ALWAYS AHEAD
The Friendly Midland Red

The faces of "Midland Red". The Birmingham & Midland Motor Omnibus Company, whatever their merits, were a rather greedy concern, gobbling up small fry and attaining a near-monopoly of their operating area. Formed in 1904, half their shares were purchased by the Great Western & London Midland Railways in 1930. Their very size and outlook, though, encouraged their building unusual and interesting vehicles.

The chassis is of an SOS "M" (Madam) class of 1929, which, although strictly speaking buses, were often pressed into use as relief coaches. They represented the first attempt to woo lady passengers with 'lazy' springing and soft seats. HA 4951, (behind the chassis) has a Ransomes body.

AHA 608 below was built in 1935 as one of the LRR (Low Rolls Royce) class fitted with Short Brothers coach bodies. The whole class of 30 were converted to buses during World War II. Standing here at Cheltenham 608 is bound for Wolverhampton.

Midland Red SOS "M"

Midland Red AHA 608

313 was completed in 1940 to full pre-war specification with a Brush 38 seat body on an SON (Saloon Onward) chassis. Here the vehicle is being driven by one of a number of lady drivers (replacing men called up for military service) and has its headlights so masked as to be totally useless. The white paint on the wings was supposed to make the vehicle more visible at night or in fog. Many a cyclist, though, was to see them too late!

The inclusive tours run by 'The Red' were, in their day, highly spoken of both within and without the trade, although by the late 1950s, possibly because customer loyalty was on the wane (with irregular bus services due to staff shortages and antique machines spoiling their reputation) the drivers no longer conveyed the panache of being la creme de la creme.

423, with her art deco radiator grill stands outside Digbeth en route to Bournemouth. Utilizing a 'K' type diesel this ONC (Onward Coach) type was fitted with a Duple body and built in 1939, was not withdrawn until 1960.

KHA 352's number will seem familiar to many tour passengers of the 1950s for her chassis was of the 1950 Duple-bodied C2 class, rejuvenated in 1962 with this Plaxton Embassy body.

When Midland Red brought out their 1958 tour brochure they laid considerable weight upon the 'dependability' of their touring vehicles. The C2, KHA 349 seen at Matlock, was already eight years old and her Duple body was showing signs of wear, while UHA 253, seen at Penzance Bus Station in 1961, was four years younger. In fact 253's Alexander-built body was so good she remained in service until 1966 when the design was long outmoded.

Rural England were a company that deserved a better end than they had. Their directors, George Finlay and Edward Holland were two of the entrepreneurial 'pirate' busmen that served London so well. This leaflet, dated 1 May 1928, gives some idea of their enthusiasm, the vehicle depicted being one of their beautiful Strachan & Brown bodied 20-seater Studebakers. Like Gladwyns they had a penchant for imitation wood finish, below the waist being painted to resemble grained walnut and above yellow; a black roof adding to the effect. Initially they worked with Red and White exchanging passengers at Gloucester but in 1929 Red & White commenced services direct and Rural England, unable to withstand a fares battle were liquidated a year later.

Rural England Motor Coaches, Ltd.
— BROWN COACHES —

All Communications to be addressed to Head Office
R.C.M.C. Ltd., General Auto Services, Uxbridge Road, Shepherds Bush Green, London.
Phone Park 9781
R.E.M.C. Ltd., Offices: 19, The Promenade, next to the Y.M.C.A., Cheltenham. Phone 3830

GO BY ROAD   GO BY ROAD

Super Luxury   Saloon Coaches

REGULAR DAILY SERVICE RAIN OR SHINE—SUNDAYS INCLUDED

TO and FROM

Three Times Daily. **GLOUCESTER CHELTENHAM** Three Times Daily.

OXFORD

AND

SWIFT SAFE SURE **LONDON** SWIFT SAFE SURE

MAIDENHEAD, HENLEY, BENSON, WITNEY, BURFORD, NORTHLEACH

Fare 9/- Single	Depart **GLOUCESTER** From 68, Southgate Street. Perks Transport. Phone 2650. H. L. Carter, Corner Woster and Northgate Street. Phone 3245.	8.15 a.m. 10.30 a.m. 4.30 p.m.	Fare 15/- Return

Fare 8/6 Single	Depart **CHELTENHAM** From Clarence Street.	8.45 a.m. 11.0 a.m. 5.0 p.m.	Fare 14/- Return

Single 5/6 4/6 3/9	DEPART Oxford for London 10.25 a.m. 12.40 p.m. 6.40 p.m. Oxford for Gloucester 12.45 p.m. 4.15 p.m. 7.45 p.m. Oxford for Cheltenham ,, ,, ,, From Acotts, 124, High Street. Phone 2082.	Return 10/- 8/6 7/-

Departing from **LONDON** 10 a.m. 2 p.m. 5 p.m.

General Auto Services Garage. Next to Central London Railway, Shepherds Bush.
Greyhound Motors, 229, Hammersmith Road. Near Kings Theatre.

All Coaches Arrive in London—
Hammersmith Broadway, " George Hotel." Opposite District Railway.
" General Auto Services Garage." Next to Central London Railway, Shepherds Bush.
Where Trains and Buses leave for all parts of Central London and Beyond

FOR INTERMEDIATE FARES AND TIMES APPLY TO YOUR NEAREST BOOKING OFFICE
Children under 12 half fare.   To Avoid Confusion when Booking Always Mention the Brown Coach.
All seats to be Booked and Paid for in advance at the Company's Booking Offices—P.T.O.

— Also at —

A halt is made at "The White Hart Hotel," Dorchester-on-Thames, where Refreshments may be obtained without delay. This Hotel was used in the days of the Horse Coaches for the same purpose. It is noted for its quaint interior and Scenic surroundings and has been the oasis for the weary traveller approximately since the 14th century.
All Tickets are issued subject to the conditions printed on the back of this leaflet.   P.T.O.

Make No Mistake When Booking
THE RURAL ENGLAND MOTOR COACHES, LTD.,
ARE THE BROWN COACHES.
P.T.O.

55

Even with the elimination of Rural England and various other independents, Oxford still remained quite well served by coaches, its bus station is here host to a Beadle-Commer chassisless coach of Timpsons (themselves far from independent) one summer's day. Some years earlier a rather dour Leyland of South Midland waits the arrival of its passengers.

SOUTH MIDLAND
MOTOR SERVICES LTD.

DAILY Coach Services

TO AND FROM

LONDON
SLOUGH, MAIDENHEAD, HENLEY

OXFORD

WOODSTOCK	CHIPPING NORTON
MORETON-IN-MARSH	BROADWAY
EVESHAM	PERSHORE

WORCESTER

SOUTH MIDLAND
MOTOR SERVICES LTD.
lll St. ALDATE'S STREET, OXFORD
'Phone—Oxford 4138-4139

ALLCHINS
LUXURY COACHWAYS

REGULAR
DAILY SERVICES
FROM

OXFORD

Victoria Booking Office
Vauxhall Bridge Road
SW1

Any self-respecting honeymoon couple based in London really ought from 1933 to 1970 to have gone to Clacton, for then they would have been able to ride on the red vehicles of Suttons Crossley Coaches; one of the companies who always seem to have tried to offer just a little more to their passengers. During the war Suttons saw a number of their vehicles commandeered and, of course, neither honeymooners or anyone else fancied a holiday on the South East coast, but their remaining vehicles transported workers to airfields being constructed, and later took German prisoners-of-war from their primeval squalid camps to work on the fields, a far cry from their normal work for both coaches and men. However, Suttons by good judgement were able to obtain extremely early delivery (1946) of six new Duple-bodied coaches, other carriers were to be less successful. Three photographs will give the flavour of Suttons fleet. OTW is one of the 1946 AEC Regal/Duple intake. Behind is a Harrington bodied coach of Grey Green (SJJ 313) leaving the Regal looking a little dated. VVW 532 is a great contrast, a Duple-bodied Leyland Royal Tiger of 1953. In 1962 Suttons took delivery of a quite different vehicle to their Royal Tigers and Reliances in the shape of a Ford, albeit still Duple-bodied; the following year that tradition was lost with the entry of a Plaxton body into the fleet. For various reasons, the last of Sutton's Crossley Coaches (actually a Ford) clattered off up the road in September 1979 and only memories and photographs remain, as is so with too many independents.

Look for the Red Coaches!

A visit to Norwich would be an essential requirement for any well-travelled honeymoon couple, if only to visit the Mann Egerton coachworks in the town, although the Austin CXB shown here looks (indeed, as it were, 'in the flesh' looked) somewhat 'gone wrong' around the front. But no doubt the workmanship was excellent; MAF 544 still exists, 40 years later, albeit rather unloved.

The first appearance is not deceptive

A fine new coach takes anyone's eye but what is it going to look like, and sound like, in say two years' time?

If in fact a coach is to retain its pristine smartness over a long period and maintain a pleasing silence it must be built from the most durable kinds of materials; neither the construction nor the workmanship must be skimped in any way.

Mann Egerton 31-seater Norfolk Coach on Austin chassis. It embodies the Mann Egerton forward-control conversion, which permits a full—fronted coach on modern lines.

These requirements are met fully in all Mann Egerton Coaches; the timber is well seasoned—a guarantee against warping; steel sections judiciously introduced give additional strength; the final exterior finishes are of special synthetic enamels and varnishes; all the interior appointments are of the best quality, while fittings, such as door locks, are practical and foolproof. Highly skilled coachbuilders, who know their job from A to Z, carry out the work.

Here then is your assurance that Mann Egerton Norfolk Coaches will stand up to constant wear and tear and still look the part after thousands of miles of operational service.

Modern Coachbuilding by | **Mann Egerton**

MANN EGERTON & CO, LTD., NORWICH · Telephone: Norwich 20291 · LUXURY COACHES AND BUSES

The route network of Lincolnshire Road Car in 1935 was quite remarkably complex, particularly when it is remembered that most of this predominantly agricultural area was incredibly depressed; farm labourers even as late as the 1940s having to put their children 'in care', obviously if they had to abandon children due to terribly low wages a weekly bus to market was often more than they could afford.

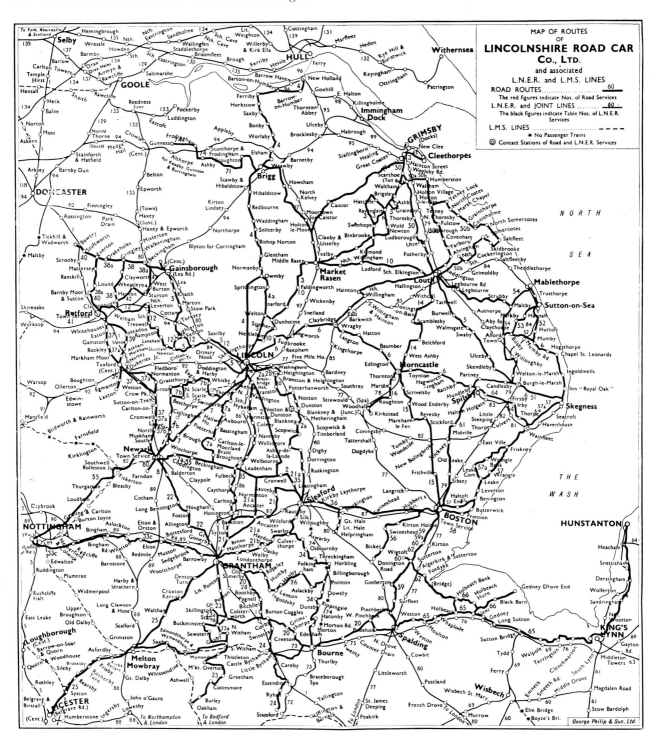

The growth of road travel since the Great War has done more to alter our ingrained habits and customs and to increase our knowledge of our own countryside than was accomplished in the whole of the preceding century. It is indeed an age of travel, and the rapid development of road traffic has no other parallel in history. Rich and poor, young and old, can all take an equal share in the benefits to be derived for mind and body from road travel. The two slogans of the road - "Blow the cobwebs away" and "See your own countryside" - make an invaluable and irresistable appeal.

Our specialized knowledge and experience is at your service, and we hope that we may often have the pleasure of your company on "the open road".

LINCOLNSHIRE ROAD CAR CO.LTD.,
BRACEBRIDGE HEATH,
LINCOLN.

Chapter Six

Coaching Choice

A day at the races once provided coach operators with a nice layer of butter on the bread of day to day operation. In 1921 Brooklands wooed customers whereas 35 years later Epsom Tours operated excursions to all major horse-racing circuits. Doncaster Corporation ran a Leyland on their 6d (2½p) return special to the racecourse in the 1930s, Leon (also of Doncaster) made more of an outing with his Daimler in the 1950s, while Cronshaw of Hendon was even more upmarket with his Duple Yeoman bodied Ford 570 of 1961.

RACE MEETINGS

Excursions will be operated throughout the year to the following Race Meetings.

ASCOT	6 3	HURST PARK	...	3 9
(Gold and Hunt Cup Days 7 6)		KEMPTON PARK	...	3 9
BRIGHTON	7 6	LEWES (Sats. 8/-)	...	7 6
(Saturdays 8/-)		LINGFIELD ...	...	5 3
FOLKESTONE ...	8 -	NEWBURY ...	...	8 9
		NEWMARKET	...	7 9
FONTWELL	8 3	PLUMPTON ...	...	6 9
(Whit-Sat. and Mon. 8/9)		SANDOWN ...	...	3 9
GOODWOOD	10 3	WYE	...	8 -

Special fares from Dorking :

FONTWELL—7/6   GOODWOOD—8/9   NEWMARKET—8/6

All coaches depart from Waterloo Road, Epsom, and in certain instances pick up "on route" (enquire for details). Coaches depart from all race courses half-an-hour after last race. Seats are numbered for the Royal Ascot and Goodwood meetings only.

Rowley Course, Newmarket. Leyland OPD 2/1 with Northern Counties 53 seat body, new to PMT in 1949, owned by Harris, t/a Progressive Cambridge, on hire to ECOC on service from Railway Station. Smart in invory and white with red lettering.

"Burtons go racing" at Rowley Mile Course, Newmarket. Identical to the two SB's purchased new, this example was a Duple 38 seater but new to the well known Cronshaw, Hendon fleet. Seen on hire to Eastern Counties for transport of punters to and from the railway station.

National Omnibus & Transport were to become one of the largest coaching groups in the country. When one looked at their latest vehicles it was salutory to reflect that not only did they operate char-a-bancs but before that, the largest fleet of steam buses ever built.

NATIONAL
CHAR-A-BANCS

ⅢⅢ LYNTON & LYNMOUTH ⅢⅢ

Via Amesbury, Taunton and Barnstaple.
This Service will operate direct whenever possible, but in certain circumstances
it may be necessary for Passengers to change at BARNSTAPLE.
★Commencing **Easter Thursday, 24th March** (see column adjoining map).
Depart **VICTORIA COACH STATION 9.0 a.m.**

LYNTON   from Lynmouth

Halting on the Outward
Journey :
OAKLEY
AMESBURY (1 hour, Lunch)
TAUNTON (½ hour, Tea).
BARNSTAPLE
Arrive **LYNTON 8.28 p.m.**

Returning from :
LYNTON (E. E. Porter,
Coach House) **9.0 a.m.**
BARNSTAPLE
(National Office, The Strand)
10.3 a.m.
TAUNTON (White's
Hotel) **1.7 p.m.**

Halting on the Homeward
Journey :
TAUNTON (1 hour, Lunch)
AMESBURY
OAKLEY (½ hour, Tea).
Arrive **LONDON**
Victoria Coach Station,
8.16 p.m.

FARES   †Supplement to be paid at Railway
Station if returning by Train.

	Single	Return	Adult	Child
LYNTON for LYNMOUTH	20/—	37/6	*8/—	1/6
BARNSTAPLE - -	20/—	37/6	5/9	6d.
TAUNTON - -	15/—	27/6	6/3	1/3

*Via Barnstaple & Southern or Gt. Western Railways, or via Western National & Minehead (G.W.R.)
†Railway Facilities see column adjoining map.
Agent for
THE SOUTHERN NATIONAL OMNIBUS Co., Ltd., E. E. Porter, Coach House, Lynton.
Telephone : Lynton 2.

ⅢⅢⅢⅢⅢ MINEHEAD ⅢⅢⅢⅢⅢⅢⅢ

Via Amesbury, Taunton and Watchet.
★Commencing **Easter Thursday, 24th March** (See column adjoining map).
This Service will operate direct whenever possible, but in certain circumstances
it may be necessary for Passengers to change at TAUNTON.

Depart
VICTORIA COACH STATION 9.0 a.m.

Halting on the Outward Journey :
OAKLEY
AMESBURY (1 hour, Lunch).
TAUNTON (½ hour, Tea).
Arrive **MINEHEAD 6.16 p.m.**

Returning from
MINEHEAD (National Office,
2, The Avenue) **11.0 a.m.**
TAUNTON (White's Hotel) - **1.7 p.m.**
Halting on the Homeward Journey :
TAUNTON (1 hour, Lunch).
AMESBURY
OAKLEY (½ hour, Tea).
Arrive **LONDON**
Victoria Coach Station **8.16 p.m.**

FARES   †Supplement to be paid at Railway
Station if returning by Train.

	Single	Return	Adult	Child
TAUNTON - -	15/—	27/6	6/3	1/3
MINEHEAD - -	17/6	32/6	5/6	6d.

Children under 14, two-thirds Adult Fare. †Railway Facilities see column adjoining map.
THE WESTERN NATIONAL OMNIBUS Co., Ltd., 2, The Avenue, Minehead.
Telephone : Minehead 190.

National
FOR COMFORT

ⅢⅢⅢⅢⅢ ST. IVES ⅢⅢⅢⅢⅢⅢ

Via Okehampton, Launceston, Bodmin, Truro, Redruth, Camborne and Hayle.
★Commencing **Easter Thursday, 24th March** (See column adjoining map).
This Service will operate direct whenever possible, but in certain
circumstances it may be necessary for passengers to change at ST. ERTH.

Depart
VICTORIA COACH STATION 8.30 a.m.
Halting on the Outward Journey :
OAKLEY
YEOVIL (¾ hour, Lunch).
OKEHAMPTON (½ hour, Tea).
TRURO
Arrive **ST. IVES 10.44 p.m.**

Returning from   a.m.
ST. IVES (National Office, Station Hill) **7.50**
TRURO (National 'Bus Office) - **9.5**
Halting on the Homeward Journey :
LAUNCESTON
HONITON (¾ hour, Lunch).
SALISBURY (½ hour, Tea).
OAKLEY
Arrive **LONDON**
Victoria Coach Station **10.19 p.m.**

FARES   †Supplement to be paid at Railway
Station if returning by Train.

	Single	Return	Adult	Child
OKEHAMPTON -	24/—	46/—	3/3	6d.
LAUNCESTON -	24/—	46/—	6/3	6d.
BODMIN - -	25/6	48/—	9/—	1/—
TRURO - -	27/6	50/—	11/—	2/—
ST. IVES - -	27/6	50/—	13/9	3/6

Children under 14, two-thirds Adult Fare. † Railway Facilities see column adjoining map.
THE WESTERN NATIONAL OMNIBUS Co., Ltd., Station Hill, St. Ives.
Telephone : St. Ives 216.

ⅢⅢⅢⅢⅢⅢ NEWQUAY ⅢⅢⅢⅢⅢⅢ

Via Okehampton, Launceston, Bodmin, Indian Queen and St. Columb.
★Commencing **Easter Thursday, 24th March** (See column adjoining map).

Depart **VICTORIA COACH STN., 8.30 a.m.**

This Service will operate direct whenever possible, but in certain circumstances it may be necessary for passengers to change at INDIAN QUEEN.

Halting on the Outward Journey :
OAKLEY
YEOVIL
(¾ hour, Lunch)
OKEHAMPTON
(½ hour, Tea)
Arrive **NEWQUAY 9.21 p.m.**

Returning from **NEWQUAY**
(National Office, 20, East St.) **9.15 a.m.**
Halting on the Homeward Journey :
LAUNCESTON
HONITON
(¾ hour, Lunch)
SALISBURY
(½ hour, Tea)
OAKLEY
Arrive **LONDON**
Victoria Coach Stn. **10.19 p.m.**

The Famous
Cornish Resort.

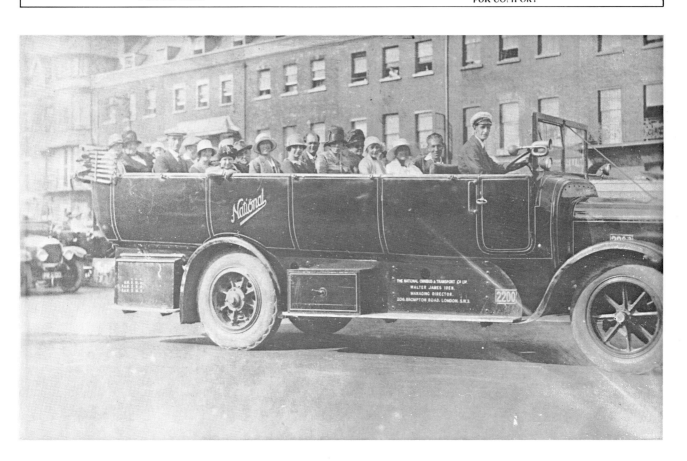

NEWQUAY

FARES   †Supplement to be paid at Railway
Station if returning by Train.

	Single	Return	Adult	Child
OKEHAMPTON -	24/—	46/—	3/3	6d.
LAUNCESTON -	24/—	46/—	6/3	6d.
BODMIN - -	25/6	48/—	9/—	1/—
NEWQUAY - -	27/6	50/—	11/—	2/—

Children under 14, two-thirds Adult Fares. †Railway Facilities see column adjoining map.
THE WESTERN NATIONAL OMNIBUS Co., Ltd., 20, East Street, Newquay.
Telephone : Newquay 72.

National
FOR COMFORT

South Wales Transport were a large quasi-private concern (actually an autonomous part of the British Electric Traction Group) and it is interesting to note this timetable is dated March 16th, 1918, a time when few "coach" services ran.

Services inside Llanelly were provided by the tramcars of the Llanelly & District Power Supply Company, one of whose cars is seen approaching Stepney Street in 1911. Later the electricity company were to operate both trolley buses and coaches - an AEC Regal is seen here, but their advertising is particularly interesting. In 1952 they fell into the hands of South Wales Transport.

THE facilities afforded by this service to West Wales are both unique and popular, as the time saved (as well as lower cost) is worth consideration, and since it was inaugurated the number of passengers using it has steadily increased. Passengers never tire of travelling by road through beautiful rural Wales and this service provides the only means of doing this in splendid comfort. Luxurious coaches are employed, manned by expert drivers who have been specially trained for the routes. To those who appreciate gorgeous scenery we can commend this service, as it passes through areas that inspired men such as George Borrow, and the delights are still unpolluted. This service provides the means of a holiday in West Wales at a very low cost, as the tickets issued enable passengers to return just when they want to. No restrictions are imposed, except that the office must know when to reserve the accommodation. Light luggage may be taken without any charge being made. We strongly invite you to try the service. Full particulars as to fares, times, etc., may be obtained from your local booking office.

South Wales Transport Co., Ltd.

MOTOR COACH SERVICE

BETWEEN

LLANELLY, PWLL, BURRY PORT, & PEMBREY.

(TOWN HALL)   TIME TABLE from MARCH 16th, 1918.   (COMMERCIAL ARMS)

Monday, Tuesday, Wednesday & Friday Service.

	am	pm	pm	pm	pm	pm	pm	pm
Llanelly Town Hall ....dep	10 40	12 10	1 45	3 15	4 45	6 15	7 45	9 30
Pwll, Colliers' Arms..............	10 55	12 25	2 0	3 30	5 0	6 30	8 0	9 45
Burry Port, Railway Hotel........	11 10	12 40	2 15	3 45	5 15	6 45	8 15	10 0
Pembrey, Commercial Arms...arr	11 20	12 50	2 25	3 55	5 25	6 55	8 25	10 10
Pembrey, Commercial Arms...dep	11 25	1 0	2 30	4 0	5 30	7 0	8 30	10 20
Burry Port, Railway Hotel........	11 35	1 10	2 40	4 10	5 40	7 10	8 40	10 30
Pwll, Colliers' Arms..............	11 50	1 25	2 55	4 25	5 55	7 25	8 55	10 45
Llanelly Town Hall ....arr	12 5	1 40	3 10	4 40	6 10	7 40	9 10	11 0

Sunday Service.

	pm	pm	pm	pm	pm	pm
	1 45	3 15	4 45	6 15	7 45	9 30
	2 0	3 30	5 0	6 30	8 0	9 45
	2 15	3 45	5 15	6 45	8 15	10 0
	2 25	3 55	5 25	6 55	8 25	10 10
	2 30	4 0	5 30	7 0	8 30	10 20
	2 40	4 10	5 40	7 10	8 40	10 30
	2 55	4 25	5 55	7 25	8 55	10 45
	3 10	4 40	6 10	7 40	9 10	11 0

Thursday and Saturday Service.

	am	pm	pm	pm	pm	pm	pm	pm	pm	pm	pm	pm	pm	pm
Llanelly Town Hall ....dep	10 40	12 15	1 45	2 30	3 15	4 0	4 45	5 30	6 15	7 0	7 45	8 30	9 15	10 0
Pwll, Colliers' Arms..............	10 55	12 30	2 0	2 45	3 30	4 15	5 0	5 45	6 30	7 15	8 0	8 45	9 30	10 15

Julius & Lockwood offered a service of "All Weather' coaches to Brighton back in the 1920s, but some years later even more spectacular vehicles were to be found at this seaside resort, for every year the British Coach Rally took place and every operator worthy of the name showed off his latest little gem.

Winning a 'pot' or two was worthy of a boast or two, Harringtons having no compunction whatsoever in blowing their own trumpet in 1963. A late survivor is seen in 1990, undergoing restoration.

Harringtons had always been in the forefront of coach design, offering not only a certain flair but consistently good quality workmanship. The seasonal summer surge in orders has always bedevilled coachbuilders; came winter workpeople were laid off by some companies and new engaged in the summer, giving great problems with quality control.

the
Harrington
GRENADIER 36

NEWS FLASH !
Yelloway Motor Services Ltd., with Harrington Cavalier 36, overall winner (National Coach of 1963) at National Coach Rally, Blackpool. Award—Blackpool Challenge Trophy.

The elegant Harrington Grenadier 36' all-metal coach body, 36' long 8' 2½" wide has a maximum seating capacity for 51 passengers.
Full-height double windscreens, wide fixed windows with forced ventilation and other luxury features combined with the sweeping lines of the Grenadier ensure that this latest Harrington design is once again
—ONE STEP AHEAD

Thomas Harrington Ltd
SACKVILLE WORKS, OLD SHOREHAM ROAD, HOVE, SUSSEX, ENGLAND
TELEPHONE: HOVE 37555-6-7   TELEGRAMS: VEHICLES BRIGHTON
S P E C I A L I S T S   I N   C O A C H W O R K   F O R   S I X T Y - F I V E   Y E A R S

Chapter Seven

Coaching Away

Almost forgotten now are the myriad of 'short sea crossings', often using interesting aircraft, that had their heyday in the 1950s and 1960s. At the time this advertisement was running Air France was operating Viscount aircraft and Caravelle on 65 minute flights from London Airport to Paris (Orly) with 'The Epicurean' providing meals par excellence. Skyways service which began on 30 September 1955 was, however, cheap, although the East Kent vehicles used were often saddled with the truly awful dual purpose seats favoured by Park Royal.

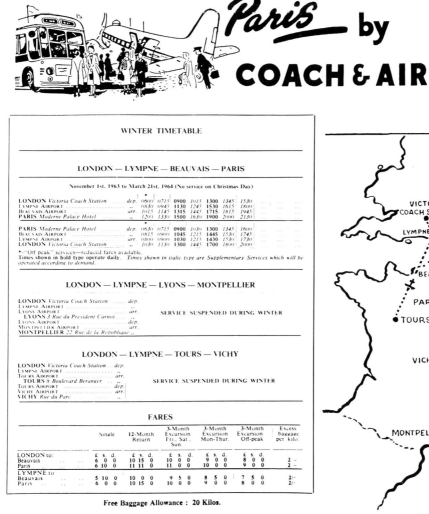

Paris by COACH & AIR

WINTER TIMETABLE

LONDON — LYMPNE — BEAUVAIS — PARIS

November 1st, 1963 to March 21st, 1964 (No service on Christmas Day)

		0600	0715	0900	1015	1300	1345	1530
LONDON *Victoria Coach Station*	dep.	0600	0715	0900	1015	1300	1345	1530
LYMPNE AIRPORT	..	0830	0945	1130	1245	1530	1615	1800
BEAUVAIS AIRPORT	arr.	1015	1145	1315	1445	1715	1815	1945
PARIS *Moderne Palace Hotel*	..	1200	1330	1500	1630	1900	2000	2130
PARIS *Moderne Palace Hotel*	dep.	0630	0715	0900	1030	1300	1345	1600
BEAUVAIS AIRPORT	..	0815	0900	1045	1215	1445	1530	1745
LYMPNE AIRPORT	arr.	0800	0900	1030	1215	1430	1530	1730
LONDON *Victoria Coach Station*	..	1030	1130	1300	1445	1700	1800	2000

*"Off peak" services—reduced fares available.
Times shown in bold type operate daily. Times shown in italic type are Supplementary Services which will be operated according to demand.

LONDON — LYMPNE — LYONS — MONTPELLIER

LONDON *Victoria Coach Station*	dep.
LYMPNE AIRPORT	..
LYONS AIRPORT	arr.
LYONS *3 Rue du President Carnot*	..
LYONS AIRPORT	dep.
MONTPELLIER AIRPORT	arr.
MONTPELLIER *22 Rue de la Republique*	..

SERVICE SUSPENDED DURING WINTER

LONDON — LYMPNE — TOURS — VICHY

LONDON *Victoria Coach Station*	dep.
LYMPNE AIRPORT	..
TOURS AIRPORT	arr.
TOURS *8 Boulevard Beranger*	..
TOURS AIRPORT	dep.
VICHY AIRPORT	arr.
VICHY *Rue du Parc*	..

SERVICE SUSPENDED DURING WINTER

FARES

	Single	12-Month Return	3-Month Excursion Fri., Sat., Sun.	3-Month Excursion Mon.-Thur.	3-Month Excursion Off-peak	Excess baggage per kilo.
	£ s. d.	£ s. d.	£ s. d.	£ s. d.	£ s. d.	
LONDON to:						
Beauvais	6 0 0	10 15 0	10 0 0	9 0 0	8 0 0	2 -
Paris	6 10 0	11 11 0	11 0 0	10 0 0	9 0 0	2 -
LYMPNE to						
Beauvais	5 10 0	10 0 0	9 5 0	8 5 0	7 5 0	2/-
Paris	6 0 0	10 15 0	10 0 0	9 0 0	8 0 0	2/-

Free Baggage Allowance : 20 Kilos.

Operators :

East Kent Road Car Co. Ltd. & Skyways Coach Air Ltd.

Bookings & Enquiries apply

TOURS DEPARTMENT,
VICTORIA COACH STATION, S.W.1

ENQUIRIES ONLY :—Telephone SLOane 3466

Coach services have always been vital to transport passengers from air termini to airports or for internal airport services. Vehicles, obviously, have varied enormously; the Hants & Dorset Leyland TD1 photographed in 1948 at Bournemouth bus station was used in connection with BOAC flights to Hurn Airport near Christchurch after having served in London during a vehicle shortage. The Bedford-Duple coach was normal for London Airport connections (albeit larger luggage lockers were fitted) while B.E.A., who used London Transport as main contractors, operated a fleet of AEC Regal IV chassis fitted with Park Royal 1½ decker bodies. Built between 1952 and 1953 they had box dimensions of 30' (9.14 m) x 8' (2.44 m), carried 37 passengers and, utilizing the boot under the upper deck, could swallow any amount of luggage.

Tours of airports always have been liked, this one dates back to 1956 and was offered by Epsom Coaches.

THAMES VALLEY   **Fare 5/9 (inclusive**
(via Windsor and London Airport)   **of Guide Fees)**
Route—Chertsey, Runnymede, Windsor (tea stop), Heath Row (conducted Tour and view the airliners), Hampton Court.
Picking-up Points : Epsom, 2.15 ; Ewell, 2.25 ; Ashtead, 2.05 ; Dorking, 1.45 ; Tadworth, 1.50 ; Woodmansterne, 1.45.
Dates of operation : April 22nd; May 30th; June 22nd; July 10th, 25th; August 11th, 20th; September 2nd, 18th; October 3rd.

Prior to the inclusive tour, the well-brought-up people of the 1920s often undertook quite complex tours of Europe by train, using coaches for their excursions. The Berlin based 'Elite' company offered a combined coach trip/cruise on the Wannsee with supper thrown in. Music and dancing on board no doubt appealed to flappers.

One result of the Great War was the imbalance of females vis-a-vis males; the girls in the Nurnberg coach (below) appear to have been teachers.

The Swiss driver's kepi and severe expression distinguishes him from most other European operators, but then to go clambering up to around 8,400' with not very good brakes would breed rather a serious class of driver. (Bottom photograph)

Touring the Continent by coach did not really appeal until the late 1930s, when as the autobahn were completed so the time taken to cover European distances became more reasonable. Autobus of Cologne offered a chance for young couples to see the real Germany, not of wartime, but of pretty, clean, blonde girls and strong youths tanned by the sun, and a cleanliness that will never return. The coaches were magnificent and it was not until the 1960s that our manufacturers even thought of really competing.

Gruss air springs are fitted to the coach as they are on Burnell's Gilford. (Frontispiece)

Armchairs, showing linen-covered head-rest and folding-table.

Emergency exit and baggage hold.

THE ARMCHAIR MOTOR COACHES de luxe used for the long-distance tours described in this booklet embody the latest developments in chassis construction and body work. The special system of pneumatic suspension (eliminating vibration), the comfort of the armchairs, the safety glass panels at both sides of the electrically operated hood (which, even when the hood is closed, afford an unobstructed view) and many other features make these coaches THE LAST WORD IN ROAD TRAVEL.

Safety glass roof at both sides of hood, affording the passengers an unobstructed view when the hood is closed.

Allweather-hood, electrically opened and closed while driving.

Special pneumatic springs for easy riding.

AUTOBUS

34

Published by the Autobus Company, Cologne. Printed in Germany.

Before the present troubles Northern Ireland had a flourishing tourist trade and indeed there is still a strange, haunting beauty to be found. Because of the relatively short distances involved the whole of a coach tour could be leisurely; in the Uptons Tours only one hotel was used, the Marine at Ballycastle. The left hand photograph shows an Ulster Transport Authority Leyland PS2 awaiting passengers from the cross-channel steamer at Donegall Quay, Belfast - note the ingenious way of displaying the operator's name. The right hand photograph shows a trio of UTA AEC Reliances travelling southward on an Antrim Coast Road day tour in 1962, exactly as Uptons' clients did on Monday.

70

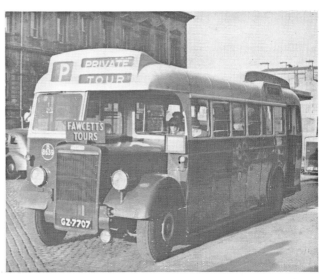

Fawcett's were, again, based at one hotel, the Royal at Portrush, an area described as "one of the finest seaside resorts in the British Isles famed for its natural loveliness". In 1968 a week cost £16. 5.0 (£16.25) without tours, £19 with, for full board, five coach outings and six evenings entertainment. Photographs, top to bottom: UTA Leyland PSI at Donegall Quay, Belfast, waiting for passengers off the cross-channel steamers, 1959. (Middle) UTA AEC Regal is seen passing through the exquisitely picturesque little village of Crawfordsburn in County Down during a day tour in 1946. (Bottom) UTA Leyland Tiger Cubs at the Slieve Donard Hotel, Newcastle, County Down in 1963. This rather fabulous hotel was originally built for the Belfast & County Down Railway in 1898.

On "General Holidays", the Belfast Omnibus Company would run excursions to all the beauty spots of Northern Ireland; in 1934 for example a trip to Lough Erne offered a cruise on the Lough and lunch at the hotel cost 2/6d (12½p). Around ten years previously McNeil of Larne has lined his fleet up outside the Laharna Hotel, Larne, prior to a day excursion; the leading vehicle is a Dennis, then a Ford model 'T' and a Maudsley.

THE BEST WAY TO TRAVEL

DROMORE GENERAL HOLIDAY

Excursion by Sun Saloon Coaches

TO

DOWNPATRICK,

ARDS PENINSULA AND BANGOR

MONDAY, 5th AUGUST, 1935.

Departing from DROMORE at 8-30a.m. arriving at Downpatrick at 9-30a.m. where a stop of one hour will be made allowing time to visit

CATHEDRAL and ST. PATRICK'S GRAVE

THEN VIA KILLYLEAGH, COMBER, AND NEWTOWNARDS TO

BALLYWALTER

ARRIVING AT 12-0 NOON

AN HOUR AND A HALF WILL BE SPENT HERE ALLOWING TIME FOR LUNCH.

Proceeding at 1-30p.m. via Greyabbey and Kircubbin to PORTAFERRY then at 3-0p.m. via Portavogie, Ballyhalbert, Ballywalter, Millisle and Donaghadee to

BANGOR

arriving about 5-0p.m.
LEAVING BANGOR AT 9-0p.m.
the homeward journey will be made via
BELFAST and LISBURN arriving at DROMORE at 10-30p.m. approx.

COACH 5/- FARE

TICKETS MAY BE OBTAINED AT B.O.C. OFFICE, DROMORE, UP TO 10-0p.m. ON
SATURDAY, 3RD AUGUST, 1935.

J. McCREA M. INST. T.
MANAGING DIRECTOR.

BELFAST OMNIBUS COMPANY, LIMITED.

Chapter Eight

Coaching South Westerly

Associated Motorways, whose address was so simply "Coach Station, Cheltenham Spa", offered probably the greatest network of services that have ever been seen in the United Kingdom, prior to the motorway age.   But for comfort, service and economy they were incomparable in any age. Whatever the rights or wrongs of their being quasi-nationalized, there is no doubt that each 'branch' added a little individuality to the tree.   The map shows just where you could go via Cheltenham, for example a 10 p.m. departure from Glasgow saw a honeymoon couple en route to Liverpool where they changed to a 7.30 a.m. departure to Cheltenham - a booked six hour run, and after a break, the 2.30 p.m. from Cheltenham would see them in Paignton at 9.34 precisely that night - all that for a mere £3.2s.2d (£3.11) single against £9 by rail.

The addresses are just one page from the booking office list; names redolent of the great days of coaching and coachmen.

Carmarthen: Morgan, Pritchard & Son, Red Street.
　　Western Welsh Omnibus Co. Ltd., Blue Street.
Cardigan: G. James, Finch Square.
Cardiff: Red & White Services Ltd., Coach Station,
　　Wood Street, Phone 23961.
　　Thomas Cook & Son Ltd., 28 High Street.
　　L. Easterbrook, Whitchurch Road P.O.
Chagford: D. B. Thomas, 1 Mill Street.
Chandlersford: Jenkins & Son, 14 The Parade.
Chard: Southern National Omnibus Co. Ltd.
Cheadle: Potteries Motor Traction Co. Ltd.
Cheltenham: Black & White Motorways Ltd., Coach
　　Station, Phone 3067, and Paris House, Phone 3060.
　　Bristol Omnibus Co. Ltd., Clarence Street.
　　Red & White Services Ltd., Phone 3047.
　　Thomas Cook & Son Ltd., 21 Promenade.
　　R. G. Badham, 102 Whaddon Road.
　　Mr. A. F. Codrington, Lyefield Road West.
　　Mr. C. R. Mullard, Tennyson Road Post Office.
　　A. L. J. Page, Edward Wilson House, Arle.
Chepstow: Red & White Services Ltd.
Chester: Crosville Motor Services Ltd., Northgate St.
Chesterfield: Ellis Travel Bureau, Holywell Street.
Chichester: Southdown Motor Services, Bus Station.
Chideock: A. S. Rendell, Post Office.
Chippenham: Rebbecks Travel Agency, Market Place.
Chipping Norton: W. Brindle, 11 High Street.
Chipping Sodbury: Dunkerley & Co. Ltd., Broad St.
Christchurch: Mrs E. G. Kingsbury, 15 Bargates
　　F. H. G. Fugatt, 96 Purewell.
　　Mr. A. Reed, 135 Barrack Road.
Church Stretton: V. C. Goatley, Sandford Avenue.
Cilfynydd: W. Brown, 18 Richard Street.
Cinderford: Red & White Services Ltd., High Street.
Cirencester: Yeoman, Miller & Co., 10 Castle Street.
　　Baily & Woods, Market Place.

Evesham: "Midland Red," High Street.
Exeter: Western National Omnibus Co. Ltd., 48/50
　　Queen Street, Phone 74191.
　　Devon General Omnibus Co. Ltd., Paul Street.
　　Airlines (Jersey) Ltd., Exeter Airport.
　　G. Dunn, 44 Paul Street.
　　Co-ordinated Road Travel Services, Alphington St.
　　Greenslades Tours Ltd., 14 Queen Street.
　　Thos. Cook & Son Ltd., 243 High Street.
　　Messrs. Park & Co. Ltd., 34 Bedford Street.
Exmouth: Greenslades Tours Ltd., Imperial Road.
　　Renwick, Wilton & Dobson, Imperial Road.
Eynsham: J. G. Pimm & Sons, Central Stores.
Falmouth: Western National Omnibus Co. Ltd.
Fareham: Hants & Dorset Motor Services Ltd.
Farnborough: Mrs. Treanor, Coach Cafe.
Faringdon: Carters', Market Place.
Farington Gurney: Matthews & Son, Duchy Garage.
Farnham: Aldershot & District Traction Co. Ltd.
Ferndale: Mrs. O. East, Darran Cafe, The Strand.
Ferndown: Ferndown Travel Bureau, Victoria Road.
Fordingbridge: A. J. and Q. Read, High Street.
Freshwater (I.O.W.) : W. G. Seldon, Station Road.
Frome: T G. Finch 23 King Street.
Gainsborough: Lincolnshire Road Car Co.
Gilfach (Bargoed): J. E. Davies, 90 Park Place.
Gillingham: Blackmore Vale Engineering Co. Ltd.
Gilwern: R. A. James, Corner Shop, Main Road.
Glastonbury: Mrs. D. M. King, 22 Magdalene Street
Gloucester: Bristol Omnibus Co. Ltd., London Road.
　　Mrs. W. Gillespie, Chelt. Road East, Post Office.
　　Thomas Cook & Son Ltd., 51 Eastgate Street.
　　Ravenshill's Ltd., Barton Street and Matson Avenue.
　　D. A. J. Mann, Longlevens.
　　Taylors Stores, Hucclecote.
Glynneath: W. Harris, 11 High Street.

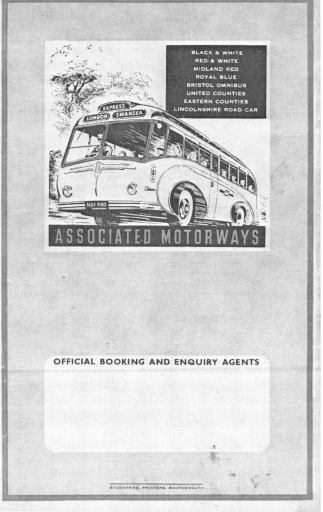

Almost a history of coaching in a few photographs. 101 with the sunshine roof was a Gardner-engined Bristol L6G of 1939 fitted with a Duple 31-seat body. JDD is also an L6G with Duple bodywork but of a curious transitional period with full front and exposed radiator. Older is this AEC Regal with a Weymann dual purpose (coach/bus) 32 seat body. Built in 1937 for the City of Oxford Motor Services Ltd., she served Black & White as a relief vehicle due to non-availability of new machines during 1950-1.

Power galore is KDF's offering with her 33 seat 1950 Willowbrook body on a Leyland Royal Tiger 9.8 litre engine. XUO 712 a 1958 Bristol MW6G with an ECW 41 seat body alongside was en route to Bournemouth. SDF was one of a batch of 1956 AEC Reliance chassis, with Willowbrook 37 seat bodywork, while, the 1954 Duple body on NDG catches the light as she leaves Cheltenham. Guy Arab LUF chassis.

The vehicles used by Black & White were magnificent, conveying a sense of welcoming to the passengers; and were always distinguishable from others of lesser ilk. It was always said that despite punishing schedules, vacancies for drivers never needed to be advertised.

DF 7840 was a 1929 Leyland Tiger TS2 with a Leyland body seating no more than 26 passengers. There was, of course, a toilet compartment and the vehicle was not only carpeted throughout, but all windows were curtained. Heaters were fitted for use in inclement weather. A steward accompanied the passengers on each trip serving hot chocolate (from a machine), ensuring paper towels were always available, and, final touch, arranging fresh flowers in the vases fitted regularly through the body. Seats were upholstered in a sumptious moquette and lighting well in advance of the norm was specially arranged so that the passengers could read the (free) newspapers available. Incidentally the condition of the tyres is interesting; one never seemed to see a Black & White with badly worn treads.

By contrast, a 1955 line-up of Black & White vehicles, all of which were to see 11 or 12 years service. The NDG series have Duple 37-seater bodies on Guy Arab LUF chassis, the PAD series on the same chassis type had Willowbrook 37 seaters.

In 1937 Weston-super-Mare was still offering itself as a resort, unlike today when hotels have become nursing homes and housing replaces the scenery at Worle and Uphill. Fares are rather higher now, and the Eastern Coachworks bodied Bristol has long gone.

Long, long before the days of television Cheddar Gorge was a sight to really thrill a typewriterist, clerk or ladies-shop assistant and to have a day out thus well justified commemorative postcards. The girls look happy enough, although the notice on the left reads "Entrance to cave, Prehistoric man on view", and that might well frighten a few!

The leaflet pre-dates the absorption of Elliott Brothers by Thomas Tilling (i.e. Western & Southern National) in 1935, the coach, No. 2863, is an ex-Western National Leyland TS2 of 1929 rebodied by Beadle in 1937.

A contrast is provided by this photograph dated 6 October 1919 showing an emergency Penzance-London bus standing outside the Red Lion, Boscawen Street, Truro during one of many railway strikes. The passengers might find it inclement on top, the driver agony with an open cab and solid tyres.

Western National

A Western & Southern National map of 1933.

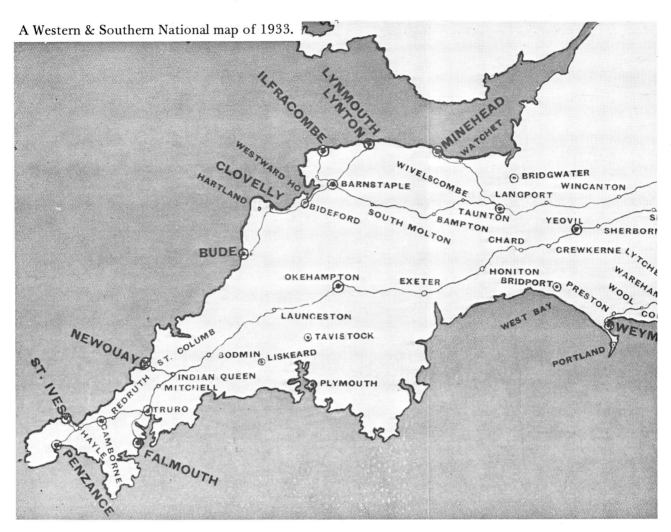

Four private hire Western National vehicles standing in Redruth.

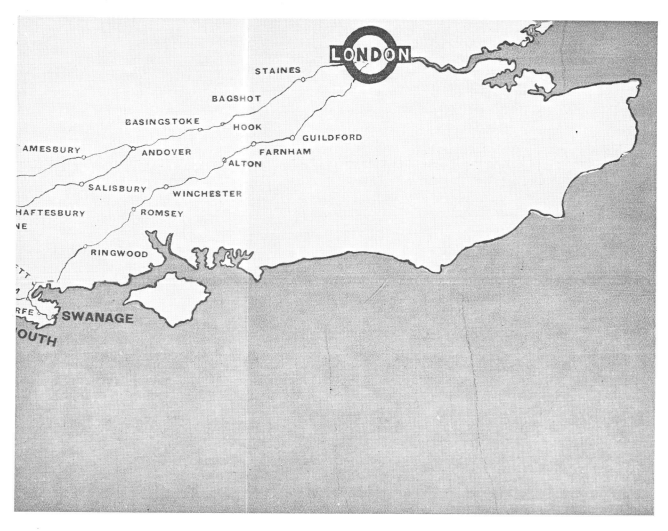

A Southern National vehicle.

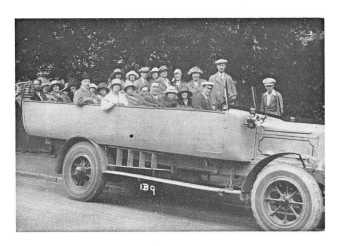

Torquay always had the reputation of being a warm, pleasant and genteel resort - the 'English Riviera'. Not unsurprisingly coaching activities played their part and this panorama of vehicles depicts a little of this. Two 'Grey Torpedo Cars', neither dated but probably 1920 and 1927, the first owned by the South Devon Garage & Motor Touring Company, the latter by The Grey Cars Ltd. Balloon tyres have appeared in this 1924 photograph, necessitating the use of a ladder to get on board. By 1954, a Duple Bedford OB of Marigold Tours prepared to leave the Torpoint ferry. Grey Cars 1960 offering (on hire to Royal Blue) shows its rather odd Manx tail, but Hansons Ford Thames/Plaxton is a long way from its Huddersfield home as it gleams in the late sunshine, the polishing marks are unkindly picked out.

One of the blandishments thrust in front of prospective coach passengers was the sheer variety in the operators' names, particularly by contrast with the four railway companies. Strawhatter derived their name from a major industry in Luton; indeed the Luton van design so commonly found now was developed to enable hats to be carried easily, a bulky but light load. Silver Cars were also called 'Good' coaches, after the proprietor. Mr. Smith's 1920 Tours were named after his Dennis vehicles, a not uncommon trait among ex-servicemen, his supreme offering being "a grand tour of nearly 80 miles" to Penzance and Land's End subject, he adds, "to sufficient passengers being available and circumstances permitting". One of the other 'Silver Queens' were involved in the rat-run to Bournemouth; noticeable in this 1929 timetable is that no arrival time is even hinted at. Disregarding the question of licences for a coachman to become a tour operator he found there were three different ways to approach the subject. First of all you arranged a more or less continuous tour of an area, Scotland, Wales or

whatever. Alternatively he could leave the transport coach at the destination complete with driver and ferry his clients around the countryside. This had the advantage of ensuring the quality of the tour was consistant, and vastly simplified hotel bookings but was expensive and tied up a vehicle. Then, too, the driver did not always have sufficient local knowledge to find alternative routes in bad weather. Thirdly the operator could always dump his clients at the hotel and leave them to sort themselves out. This wasn't really very clever (although practised) so normally 3 or 4 optional (but highly recommended) day trips were offered by arrangement with the local day tour operator - sometimes the vehicle was exclusively for the use of the party. Private hire tours where the party told the operator where they wanted to go were another matter, and, given a good driver and courier, could lead to much repeat work. It could also be a fiasco. Grey Cars were originally an independent operator but got gobbled up to become Devon General's local operators. Eventually they became responsible for all General's coaching activities.

Chapter Nine

Flicker Flashback

One of the most pleasant aspects of early coach operators was their brashness and, quite often, their imagination in offering their passengers the latest gimmick - or inventions.   Little seems to have been recorded of Trelawny Tours activities; neither have photographs been traced, but they at least tried to satisfy their customers requirements.

Know-as-you-go.   The exclusively "Silent Guide" Motor Coaching.

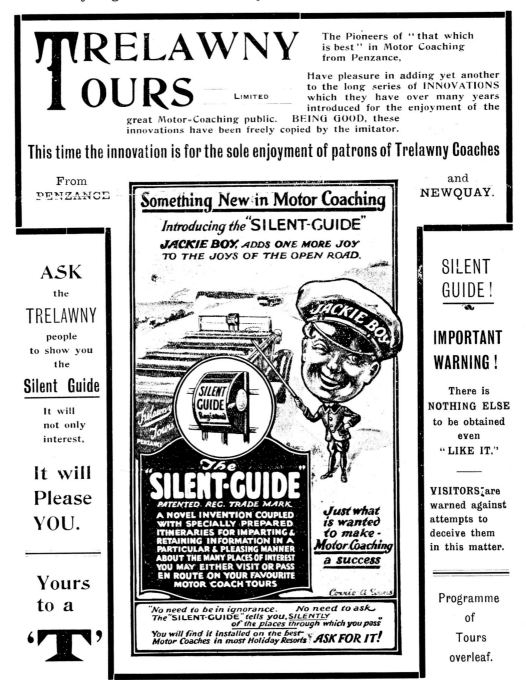

YOU WANT THE BEST—THEN BE SURE AND TOUR BY TRELAWNY.

MOTOR COACH TRAVEL

Under recent legislation recognising the national utility of Motor Coach Services, provision is made for a new method of licensing these services and vehicles. Objections may be lodged to the grant of the license which gives the necessary permission to operate certain services.

The railways are objecting to practically every motor coach service in the country, and they state as reasons that these services are unnecessary and undesirable in the public interest.

If these railway objections are upheld YOU will be deprived of the motor coach, which beats the train in COMFORT, PRICE and CONVENIENCE.

Additionally, should the railways obtain this monopoly of passenger transport, they will return again to that lethargic state from which, after the ten years' competition of motor transport, they are just emerging.

YOU PAY,
CHOOSE YOUR WAY,
ROAD OR RAIL.

Issued by The Motor Hirers' and Coach Services Association, 7a, Great Portland Street, W. (The Association of Independent Coach Operators) and Printed by Haycock Press, London.

This leaflet was part of a desperate attempt by the independant operators to survive the chill winds of 1930s regulation; most eventually succumbed to the might of the railway backed "big boys".

The manifold aspects of coaching can be summed up in these illustrations. UCOC 333, waiting departure from Cheltenham Coach Station in the late 1930s was a Daimler CF6 new in 1929 as NH9177, was withdrawn by 1940 and sold to Robertson, Leith. Originally fitted with a Crabtree 26 seat charabanc body when new to Allchin & Son, Northampton 333 passed to UCOC in November 1933.

"One return, one single to High Cliffs."

Transport humour tends to be slightly sardonic. Working on coaches has always been rather a lonely job, with little chance to regularly meet one's colleagues. The divorce rate among drivers was horrendous, many girl passengers going on holiday making their charms all too obvious. Maybe the aftermath is shown here!

After the end of World War 2 travel restrictions were progressively relaxed, although the country was under the iron grip of 'Austerity', lacking in fuel, raw materials, and the cash to pay for either. Bus services to and from factories or other places of employment received priority for petrol and diesel supplies and then the 'express coach services' with outings coming a long way behind.

New vehicles were like hen's teeth and many of the pre-war coaches, whether stored or not, were suffering from tired joints, woodworm and good old fashioned rot - but they ran!

Eastern National services B & C recommenced on 4th March 1946, using (and illustrating) 'bananas', one of which, DEV 451, is shown here new. A Bristol JO5G, she was built in 1936 and fitted with an Eastern Counties 31 seat coach body, not being withdrawn until 1957.

Britain is almost unique in Europe in that the saving, restoration and using of the highway of elderly vehicles is, if not encouraged, at least permitted. These two vehicles have Certificates of Fitness to carry fare-paying passengers. Rosie (972 ANK) is the pride of ESJ Motor Coaches of Saltash and St. Austell. They have more recent coaches for day-to-day operations, but Rosie has recently (1990) received a complete rebuild and repaint. However, even when seen here at Brunel's Moorswater Viaduct near Liskeard, Cornwall, in March 1987, it is difficult to realize her body was completed by Duple Coachworks as long ago as 1956. The chassis, a Bedford SBO, often scorned as a 'lightweight' has withstood years of salt and is still a credit to both manufacturers and operators. The Scottish Aviation bodied Tillings-Stevens GOU 732 then a mere 39 years old is seen leaving the Nag's Head, Canon Pyon, after lunch, on a Classic Coaches of Wombourne "Autumn Gold Tour of Worcester & Herefordshire" in 1988.

This classically styled Plaxton bodied Bedford SB3 belongs to the rightly named Nostalgia Unlimited Company and is seen here in Chester during 1989. This pattern of bodywork remains perhaps the most famous of all; first seen in 1952 it was still available, slightly modified, on certain Bedford chassis until at least 1972. Sadder, but facing a great future is a unique Burlingham Seagull bodied AEC Regal IV built in 1950. Rescued from the scrapyard she was once the pride of Burnhams of Worcester, and is unique insofar as the centre sliding door is a Burlingham conversion from an inward opener and the window frames are reversed to present a smoother profile and assist with mechanical cleaning - a typical touch of 'operators ingenuity'. The sterling priced notice is genuine and around 25 years old. Once a Manchester based firm, Hillcrest are still operating but tours cost somewhat more. The Hovercraft was the wonder of the age and crossing the Mersey tunnel was still a little different for our passengers of that less blase age. [12 pence = 1/-, 20/- (shillings) a UK£, so Coventry was 70p, Blackpool 50p, Rhyl 56¼p. . . and Southport 38¾p!] However even in 1990 oldfashioned unsophisticated chalk boards still serve a purpose; this was found at George Patterson & Sons' premises, Beadnell, Northumberland.

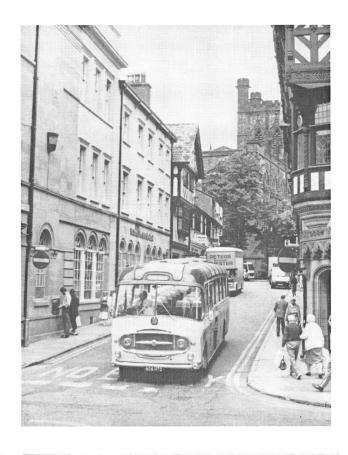

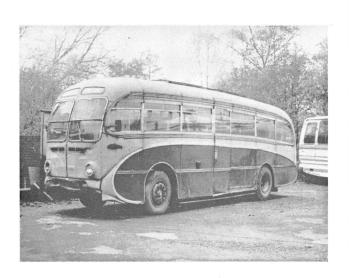

Inevitably there came the day when all that was seen of the coach was the rear end. Shapely though this may be, there must always be sadness at a parting. LTA 898, Royal Blue No. 1269 was photographed in Bournemouth during June 1981. A Bristol LL6B with a conservatively-styled Duple body she was built in 1961.

By contrast the Yeates Europa body gracing the Leyland Tiger Cub chassis of MTL 750, once the pride of "The Delaine" was ultra modern when built in 1958 and still gleams in the winter sunshine at Kidderminster, Worcs.

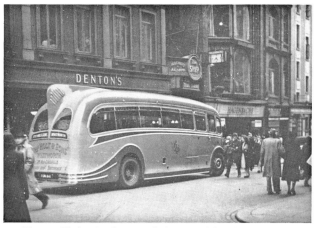

Chas. Holt & Sons of Sunnyside Garage, Whitworth, near Rochdale, were a company whose tours were never to be missed, or else how would you ride in the beautiful, if quirkily styled, Harrington body on a Leyland chassis? The rear fin, a most distinctive aspect of a Harrington body in the twenty years from 1935 was not only for ornament but carried the extractor for an advanced system of forced air ventilation.

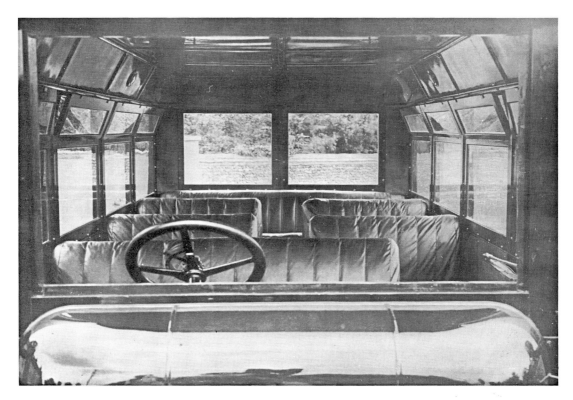

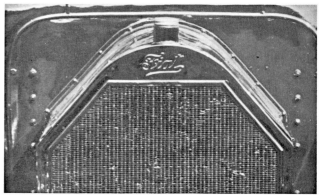

The use of converted bread vans and similar light delivery vehicles for passenger carrying is, thankfully, in decline as more attention is paid to comfort and maintainance. Often said to be the phenomenon of the eighties, these three photographs show there is nothing new under the sun, as here we have a FIAT light lorry chassis adapted to carry passenger bodywork. Although there is no clue on the photographs to show the manufacturer's name, the style is of Buckinghams in Birmingham. Pneumatic tyres are fitted and the date sometime in the early 1920s. Legally limited to 20 mph this little village operator's coach would have been nippy, comfortable, and above all easy to maintain.

Chapter Ten

Addenda

PARK ROYAL COACHWORKS LTD.

BOLTON CORPORATION
SPECIFICATION
Special 32-seater Single
Deck Omnibus Body, Composite
or Metal construction.

DESIGN
Body to be built to our Design No. 4886/1 with entrance at nearside rear and emergency door in offside front. To comply with the Ministry of Transport regulations.

CONSTRUCTION
All materials to be of the best quality and all timbers well seasoned and free from knots and shakes.

UNDER FRAME
Cross bars to be in English Ash or English Oak, reinforced each side with 1/8" nickel steel plates, bolted to gusset plates in pillars. Bottom sills - English Ash.

FRAMING
To be of seasoned English Ash strengthened with mild steel flitch and bracket plates, all framing to have two coats of lead paint. Pillars to be reinforced the full length with metal.

FLOOR
To be of 7/8" T.&G. Prime red deal boards securely screwed to bottom framing. Trap doors provided for access to gearbox, axle etc., these doors fitted with budget locks and flush lifting rings and edged with metal angle. Floorboards above converter or gearbox to be strengthened.

Cowl for differential; floor and rear wheelarches to be covered with cork carpet, cemented to floor.

Tread plates to be fitted in front of seat on offside wheelarch. Clutch and differential cowls to be supplied.

Bearers and floorboards over exhaust to be covered with Asbestos sheet.

ROOF
To be constructed with Ash hoopsticks and covered with 1/2" T.&G. Pine boards; outside to receive two coats of lead paint; all holes filled up and covered with roof canvas, bedded in white lead and gold size.

Hoopsticks strengthened with plates, turned on to cantrails and securely fixed. The front and rear ends, metal beaten to shape in aluminium.

Interior secondary roof ceiling covered with best ply, with shaped portion in aluminium. Weather guttering fitted round roof 'J' section moulding slotted for draining purposes.

Single panel sun saloon sliding roof to be fitted.

ENTRANCE
To be at rear of nearside and to be fitted with sliding type door down to bottom step. Steps covered fluted aluminium, with Ferodo treads and nosing.

This door fitted with suitable runner gear, locks and handles and spring loaded rollers and guides and track, and to comply with M.O.T. regulations.

EMERGENCY DOOR
To be at offside front of body. This door to be of full coach type hung on stout D.F. hinges and fitted with our suitable locking gear, with inside and outside handles, the latter being of sunken type and finished chromium plate.

The inner portions of the lock in black cellulose finish.

PANELS
To be of concave type in 16.G. aluminium, securely screwed to body framing, and finished at joints with cover strip and half round aluminium moulding, screwed.

Waist rails and pillars cased in 16.G. aluminium. Cut out for access to spare wheel.

WHEELARCHES
Wheelarches to be fitted to allow for the sheet metal to be finished level with the underside of floorboards.

WINDOWS

Three windows on nearside, and four on off-side to be of Widney "Ace" half frop pattern, framing to be anodically treated.

Fixed glasses to be in 3/16" English polished plate glass.

Windows in front bulkhead to be in Triplex Toughened safety glass. Approved type louvres fitted over all drop windows.

VENTILATORS

Two ventilators of approved type, to be fitted in roof with chromium plated grids.

Ventilators in top of front bulkhead, with interior baffle panel. Louvred panels in sides above windows to give permanent ventilation.

DRIVER'S CAB

To be of half type to float at radiator and side of bonnet and to have rounded front; to be built integral with the body.

Entrance to the cab to be by means of full type coach door on offside. This door hung on stout hinges and fitted with face slam locks and outside sunken handles, chromium plated.

Two glasses fitted in door, one being made to slide for signalling purposes.

Window in nearside of cab hinged to form a safety frame; two glasses fitted, one being made to slide in felt channel.

One approved type ventilator in roof of cab.

Windscreen to be of unit construction, metal framed, cellulose finished and glazed 1/4" Triplex Toughened plate, the top half being made to open outwards and secured by chromium plated locking joints. Whipple screen wiper to be fitted. Commode handles, fitted to assist entrance to cab.

Driver's seat to be adjustable. Backrest pivotted to bulkhead; cushion not to exceed 20-1/2" from floorboards.

INTERIOR FINISH & FITTINGS

Roof to be lined with scratchproof Rexine; with Walnut mouldings. Casing panels in 3-ply covered in scratchproof Rexine to match interior.

Roof underlined plywood in centre and shaped panels in 20.G. aluminium.

Two Resistoid entrance handles to be fitted to entrance.

4½" electric bell (G.E.C. L.4021) trembler type and three metal type chromium plated finish pushes (G.E.C. L.4021) fitted in roof mouldings above gangway.

Garnish rail mouldings and cappings polished Walnut, clear varnished.

All window guard and handrails covered Resistoid, shade to be approved.

Fluted aluminium kicking panels.

LIGHTING

12 interior lamps, modern circular pattern, to be fitted under parcel racks.

Also two rear roof lights and one bulkhead light to be controlled by three switches; switches to be fitted in driver's cab.

24-volt, 15-watt clear bulbs. Switches, C.A.V. Multiswitch type 86-20.

All switches and fuses to be placed on positive side.

One chassis tail light with dashboard warning "ITZIN" light in series with same.

Lamp holders to suit lamps, fitted with English Bayonet caps.

Stop lamp, your standard, with 24-volt, 6-watt bulb.

All fittings and wiring to be to your specification.

DESTINATION BOX

To be built into front of canopy. (Glass size 3' x 6-3/8" rollers over collars 3'-1.5/8". 7" centres, blinds 36" wide.)

Also above cantrail on nearside with E.&E. gears, interchangeable with your existing fittings, and blind 36" wide with provision for 48 names. Names stencilled on rear for guidance of conductor.

Boxes to be illuminated with 2 - 12 watt bulbs.

Front destination box handle to be in driver's cab.

Interior of destination box to have back frame glazed with frosted glass with a space 4" x 1", clear.

ROUTE NUMBER BOXES

To be built in roof over the front canopy. (Glasses size 10¾" wide x 10" deep. Rollers over collars 10¾" Centres 11"), also in rear of body.

Fitted with E.&E. Co.'s gears and to be interchangeable with your existing fittings.

Blinds to be fitted with provision for 35 numbers.

Boxes illuminated with one 12-watt bulb. Handle of front box to be under canopy on nearside. Both destination and route number boxes to be accessible from outside.

Numbers stencilled on rear of blinds for guidance of conductor.

SEATS

Staggered type coachbuilt pattern, with individual cushions. Cushions to have Dunlopillo fillings.

Dunlop Latex fillings to squabs. Upholstery to be in Listers "Wypdri" Eagle/F57624. Moquette throughout, with an overcovering of Connolly's hide at ends and division. Sample seat to be approved by customer. An ash tray recessed in seat backs for each passenger. See drawing 4886/1 Re: raised platform also width of body.

PARCEL RACKS

Continuous parcel racks to be fitted along either side of body, on polished brackets; underside lined Rexine to match upholstery.

WINGS

A pair of 16.G. aluminium wings with deep valances, fitted over rear wheels.

LIFEGUARDS

Single tubular type lifeguards with chromium plated mountings, to be fitted each side of vehicle detachable by wing nuts.

HEATERS

Two Clayton heaters, one mounted at front and one at rear of saloon.

PAINTING

Body to be filled up and rubbed down and the whole vehicle painted in your standard colour to choice, and highly varnished to your specification. Legal writing and transfers (supplied at cost to us) to be fixed.

GENERAL

Nesthill driving mirror No. 868 size 5½" x 3½".

Bulb horn, straight type.

Licence holder of approved type.

Lockers under rear seat with detachable seat.

Batteries to be fitted under second near and offside seats from front bulkhead.

Cast aluminium number plates at front and rear.

Two Pyrene Fire Extinguishers, chromium plated finish, one to be fitted in driver's cab and one in saloon.

A Peters collapsible blind fitted in driver's cab behind driver, in scratchproof Leather cloch with three celluloid observation slots.

Conductor's ticket box tray and ticket holder rack to your standard size.

Used ticket box.

Tool box.

Cupboard in driver's cab.

5 Sanitary handgrips fixed to roof.

Fare and stages frames.

Certificate of ownership frame.

CHASSIS

Chassis to be delivered to Manufacturer's works with cab floor fitted, tank and front wings mounted to chassis; head, side and tail lamps fitted, wired up and complete with facia board and chassis electrical equipment including electric horn and batteries.

DELIVERY

To your Garage at Bolton.

ALTERNATIVELY

Framing. To be of our patented steel framing with all joints electrically welded or where desirable, rivetted for easy replacement.

Floor bearers to be two lipped channels welded back to back, with steel flitch plate between.

Chair bars to be single lipped channel, electrically welded to floor bearers.

All steel sheets to be of best quality and all sections drawn from steel 26/23 tons tensile strength.

Well annealed rivets to be used for 3/16" cold work; any rivets of larger dimensions being put in hot.

The truss plates which run the full body length are rivetted to framework, forming an exceptionally strong girder.

The waist rail is a specially drawn section of high tensile steel running the full body length.

Packing blocks, trap framework and all body fillets to be in seasoned Teak.

All steel work is thoroughly cleaned and dipped in our special priming solution before assembly and two coats of anodite applied after assembly.

GUARANTEE

The bodywork of our manufacture carries with it our guarantee against defective material and/or workmanship for a period of 12 months or for 40,000 running miles from the date of delivery to you whichever elapses the sooner. In the case of goods not of our manufacture you are entitled to the benefit of any guarantee given to us in respect thereof.

EXTRAS

Rubber to floor in lieu of lino.

- - - - - - - - - - - - oOo - - - - - - - - - - - - -

for: PARK ROYAL COACH WORKS LTD.

Director & Sales Manager.

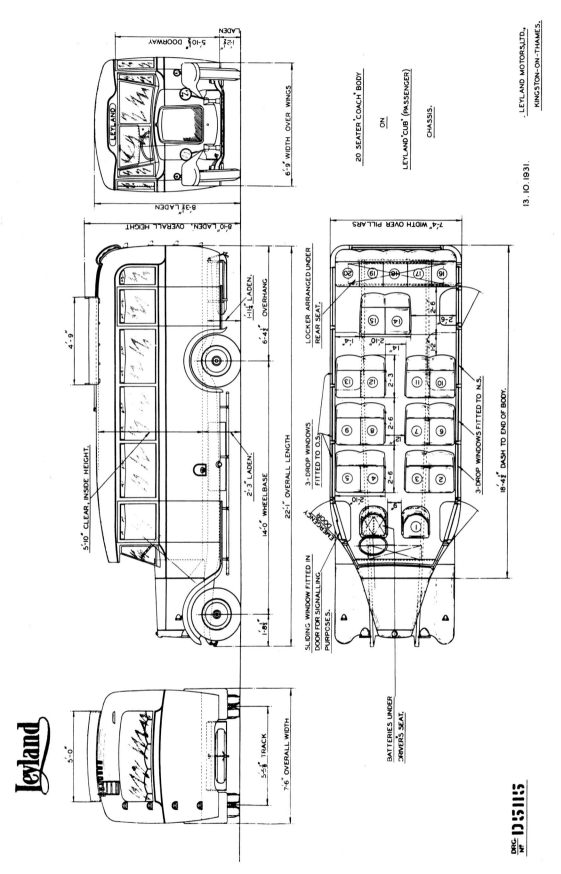

20 SEATER 'COACH' BODY

ON

LEYLAND 'CUB' (PASSENGER)

CHASSIS.

13.10.1931.

LEYLAND MOTORS,LTD.,
KINGSTON-ON-THAMES.

DRG. D5115
Nº

Two bodywork plans separated by about seven years. Leyland offered bodywork designs on virtually all their models, some were rather uninspired, one style on the 1950s Royal Tiger was desperately uncomfortable to ride in, but their 'Faringdon' bodies on PD2 chassis and the London Transport PD2/6RT(RTW) buses were masterpieces of design. The 'Cub' chassis entered service in two guises (KP2 and KP3) in 1931 and drawing D5115 shows the detail of the body offered for the KP2 14'0" wheelbase model. The chassis were built at Kingston-upon-Thames and a 6 cylinder 4.4 litre petrol engine was fitted. Lincolnshire Road Car were one of the largest operators of the type and coincidentally many of their vehicles were bodied by Brush using almost a 'crib' from the Leyland body plan.

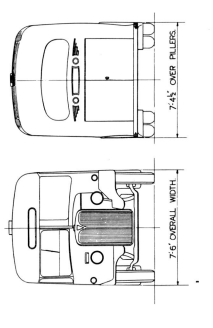

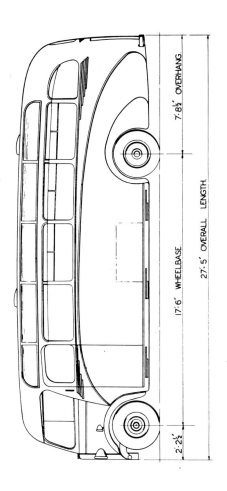

BRUSH COACHWORK Ltd.

Loughborough   England.

SEATING CAPACITY 30 PASSENGERS.

Composite construction.

Spare wheel locker with body side access.

Passenger luggage locker under rear seat with access.

Sliding door of resin-bonded metal faced plywood, moulded to shape.

Glazed louvres.   Shaped Perspex side roof quarter lights with blinds.

All windows flush fitting in pans.

Clayton Dewandre heating and ventilation.

Dwg. C.D.B. 189

General Arrangement of 30 SEATER COACH.

The Brush body drawing CDB 189 was much simpler and really designed for showing to Borough Transport Committee members than as a serious engineering drawing. After all they only wanted to see where t'brass was being spent, and did not require fine detail; that was in the Engineer's province. Shown here as suitable for mounting on an AEC Regal III chassis, similar 'General Arrangements' were available on almost any comparable chassis. Interestingly the seating is asymetrical, passengers behind the cab having 2" less legroom. The same outline of bodywork minus cantrail lights, varying amounts of trim and with the emergency door moved to the extreme rear was used for at least six bus and coach variants.

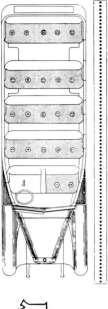

LOW-LEVEL SAFETY PASSENGER MODELS

THE introduction of Maudslay low-level safety passenger vehicles marks the culminating point in British development of luxurious, safe and comfortable motoring by coach. With well-appointed upholstery, seats arranged to afford repose, and promoting, as these new types do, a feeling of perfect confidence, both inter-urban services and long-distant touring give complete satisfaction and pleasure, consequently assuring owners an ever increasing patronage.

These vehicles operate under conditions of safety by virtue of their unusually low centre of gravity, long wheelbase and extra wide track, and the element of risk through high loading and consequent body-sway an inherent fault in many 'converted' types is entirely eliminated. Furthermore, the perfectly balanced four-wheel braking system gives the driver immediate and full control without the slightest discomfort to passengers.

Whatever degree of confidence and pleasure, however, a motor-coach may bestow by its dependability and smooth-running qualities, a factor which essentially influences the return of a good balance sheet is that of operating costs as compared with revenue, and the most economical results in fuel consumption and general upkeep can only be associated with an extended experience in passenger-vehicle construction, and by embodying well considered design in every stage of the layout.

In these respects we claim that there is no type of motor-coach on the market which has received so much detailed attention or subjected to such exhaustive trials, both on the test-bench and up and down the country, before being released, than our new safety models.

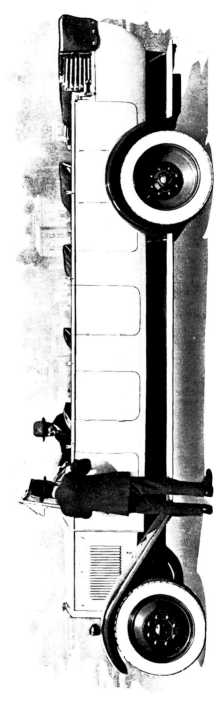

Maudslay Open-Type Safety Coach for 22 Passengers.

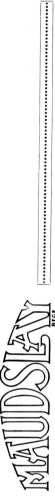

MAUDSLAY REG⁰

LOW-LEVEL SAFETY COACHES

THESE chassis are made with varying frame and engine dimensions to suit 22 Seater Open Coach, and 26-30 Seater Saloons. Also a special type is included with driver alongside engine for Saloons of large seating capacity.

INCLUDED EQUIPMENT. Electric self-starter. dynamo lighting set, one spare wheel.

TYRES. 36 in. dia. by 6 in. section straight-sided pneumatics. Twin rear.

ROAD WHEELS. Pressed-steel disc type, demountable rims. The wheels are detachable without disturbing the bearings.

FUEL SUPPLY. 18-gallon tank mounted on the offside frame-member. Constant supply at varying gradients and tank levels maintained by Autovac.

PIN AND JOINT LUBRICATION. Grease-gun system, with adaptors placed in the most accessible positions.

CHASSIS MEMBERS. Girder section, 6 in. by 3 in. or 5 in. by 3 in. Wrought-steel tubes form the cross members, and channel section for sub-frame carrying engine and gearbox. Bolts are used throughout the frame assembly.

MAIN SUSPENSION. Specially long springs working flat under load. More leaves than usual are specified for a given deflection and they are of liberal width.

STEERING.—Worm and complete wheel, non-reversible type, mounted on tapered roller bearings. 18½ in. dia. steering wheel with non-slip rim-section. All joints of phosphor-bronze cups and hardened-steel balls. The front wheels are centrally pivoted.

THE MOTOR. 100 m.m. by 130 m.m. H.P. 24-60. 110 m.m. by 130 m.m. H.P. 30-70. Four cylinder monobloc with detachable head. Five bearing crankshaft supported in top portion of crankcase. Interchangeable overhead valves. Cams of extra width, no rockers. Vertical-shaft and tappet-gear enclosed in an oil-tight and dust-proof cover. Magneto and water-pump located transversely forward of engine and well above frame.

LUBRICATION. By pressure-pump to drilled crankshaft and connecting rods for supplying main-bearings, big ends and gudgeon-pins. Oil-pipe leads to camshaft timing-bevels and bearings. An extra large filter gauze is fitted in the sump. The oil-level is readily discernible by a suitably marked dipper.

COOLING. Circulation by centrifugal pump, and air-draught by fan running on ball-bearings. Cooling surface by honeycomb type radiator of distinguished design.

CARBURETTOR.—Zenith, fitted to hot-water jacketed induction pipe.

IGNITION AND CONTROL. H.T. magneto having differentiated coupling to give fine adjustment. Spark and throttle controlled by friction-faced finger-levers neatly located above the steering wheel. The usual form of independent foot accelerator is fitted.

STARTING AND LIGHTING.—The electric self-starter and lighting dynamo are located respectively on the near and offside of the engine, and well clear of crankcase doors, the starting pinion is of the outboard bearing type. The dynamo is driven by an enclosed silent chain which is readily adjustable.

TRANSMISSION SYSTEM. CLUTCH. Inverted cone, leather-to-metal engagement. Clutch-brake to facilitate gear-changing. Thence to gearbox by intermediate shaft having a flexible coupling to the gearbox.

GEARBOX. Compact sliding-gear type providing four speeds and reverse. Ratios: First and reverse 5:1, second 2·88:1, third 1·73:1, fourth direct.

PROPELLOR SHAFT. Fitted with universal joint at the front end which articulates on enclosed ball bearings: sliding type rear joint.

FINAL DRIVE. Underslung worm, roller bearings and ball thrusts fitted throughout. Final ratio, 7:1. Drive to rear wheels through full-floating differential shafts which take no dead weight.

BRAKING SYSTEM. Brakes on all four road-wheels in addition to a foot-operated transmission set. Those on the front-wheels are servo-operated, working through the medium of the foot-brake. The rear-wheel brakes are hand-controlled, and each set is perfectly balanced. All the shoes are cam-operated, faced with friction material, and expand inside large-diameter steel drums. There are ready means for adjustment.

AXLES. FRONT. Of high-grade steel, carefully heat-treated; it is designed specially in regard to resisting the stresses of the front-wheel brakes. "I" beam section between the springs and oval beyond. The swivel-pins and arms are mounted with large-diameter roller bearings and ball thrusts.

REAR.—Chrome-nickel steel stamping, manufactured without a weld. Centre portion bored out to accommodate the worm and differential-gear casing. The unit takes imposed weight only, which permits the driving shafts and final-drive gearset to be withdrawn without use of a jack.

Maudslay, once of Coventry but later from Alcester, Warwickshire, commenced building passenger carrying vehicles in 1903, continuing until 1951, having merged with AEC and Crossley in 1948 to form Associated Commercial Vehicles. Although some AECs were subsequently badged as Maudslays this practice ceased in 1960. In due course AEC and ACV fell into the hands of Leyland, who are now merely a part of the DAF empire.

This specification appeared in 1925 when, although expensive to buy, Maudslays vehicles were highly regarded for their reliability. Incidentally they gave a twelve months guarantee on all parts except accessories, tyres and electrical fittings.

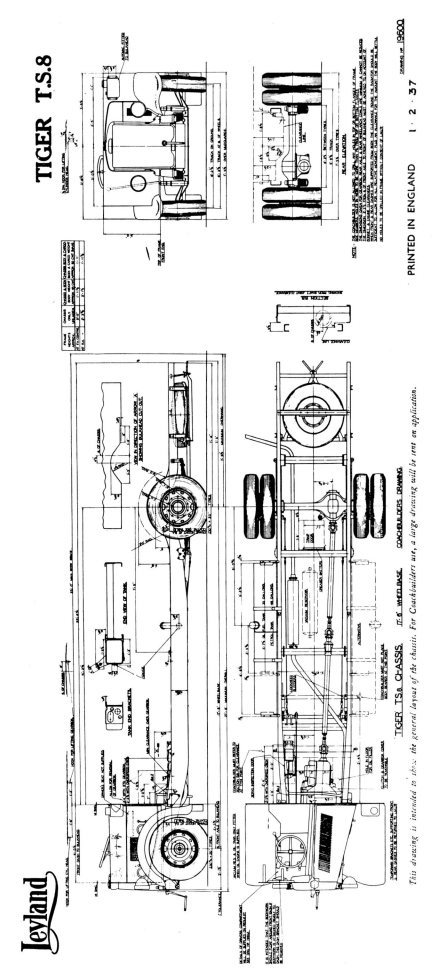

TIGER T.S.8

TIGER TS8 CHASSIS. COACHBUILDERS DRAWING.

This drawing is intended to show the general layout of the chassis. For Coachbuilders use, a large drawing will be sent on application.

Leyland

The Leyland TS8 was probably the finest of the 'Tiger' family of coaches, which originated in 1927. In general each of this TS series had a production life of no more than eighteen months, with each model representing an improvement on its predecessor. The TS1 had a wheelbase of 17'6", was powered by a 6.8 litre petrol engine, final drive being by way of a sliding mesh gearbox, underslung worm drive rear axle and vacuum servo brakes were fitted. The TS8 appeared in November 1937, gave a choice of the Mk.III variant on the 6.8 litre engine or an 8.6 litre diesel, had an updated box with constant mesh (so called 'silent') third gear, fully floating rear axle and vacuum hydraulic brakes. Production lasted until 1940.

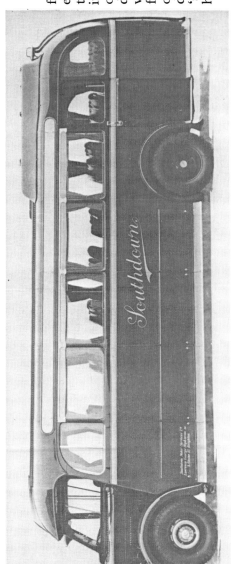

Each coach manufacturer had their own ideas on the shape
dimensions permitted by the Ministry of Transport but the
operator. It must also be added that where a firm was un
aesthetically pure lines presented on the drawing board.

Top row: Charles H. Roe, Leeds; Bellhouse Hartwell, Wes
Bottom row: Harringtons, Hove; Duple, London; Yeates, L